Play Therapy

Relationship Development Intervention

(Powerful Techniques for the Treatment of Childhood Disorders)

Clifford Loranger

Published By **Bella Frost**

Clifford Loranger

All Rights Reserved

Play Therapy: Relationship Development Intervention (Powerful Techniques for the Treatment of Childhood Disorders)

ISBN 978-1-7774403-7-4

No part of this guidebook shall be reproduced in any form without permission in writing from the publisher except in the case of brief quotations embodied in critical articles or reviews.

Legal & Disclaimer

The information contained in this book is not designed to replace or take the place of any form of medicine or professional medical advice. The information in this book has been provided for educational & entertainment purposes only.

The information contained in this book has been compiled from sources deemed reliable, and it is accurate to the best of the Author's knowledge; however, the Author cannot guarantee its accuracy and validity and cannot be held liable for any errors or omissions. Changes are periodically made to this book. You must consult your doctor or get professional medical advice before using any of the suggested remedies, techniques, or information in this book.

Upon using the information contained in this book, you agree to hold harmless the Author from and against any damages, costs, and expenses, including any legal fees potentially resulting from the application of any of the information provided by this guide. This disclaimer applies to any damages or injury caused by the use and application, whether directly or indirectly, of any advice or information presented, whether for breach of contract, tort, negligence, personal injury, criminal intent, or under any other cause of action.

You agree to accept all risks of using the information presented inside this book. You need to consult a professional medical practitioner in order to ensure you are both able and healthy enough to participate in this program.

Table Of Contents

Chapter 1: Play Therapy For Kids 1

Chapter 2: Mindfulness Meets Play Therapy 13

Chapter 3: Tools & Tips For Mindful Play 29

Chapter 4: Body, Breath, & Movement .. 40

Chapter 5: Sensory Awareness 70

Chapter 6: Imaginative Stories & Metaphors 99

Chapter 7: Play Therapy For Parents 128

Chapter 8: Benefits Of Play Therapy For Children 159

Chapter 1: Play Therapy For Kids

Play therapy is an effective method that is able to bring about changes, growth and healing for children. Before we get into the games and activities we will be doing within this book it is essential to understand the theories of the practice of play therapy. This chapter you'll discover the underlying principles of play therapy, as well as the foundational frameworks that the majority of play therapists use when dealing with children within a therapeutic environment. It will also explain what the difference is between the two different types of play that children engage in on their own. (Note that even though you are able to engage the child to engage in activities that can be positive, it shouldn't be used as a substitute of formal therapy, when necessary.

What Is Play Therapy?

Fred Rogers, host of the television show for preschoolers, Mister Rogers' Neighborhood, has been quoted in a famous quote as saying "Play is frequently discussed as if it's an escape from the seriousness of studying. For children, however, it is an essential part of learning. The work of play is really part of the childhood" (emphasis emphasis added). Rogers was conscious of an essential fact that play is how kids grow, develop, and learn. Though children often play in order to relax and have fun, it is also a potent instrument.

As per the Association for Play Therapy, play therapy is "the application of a theoretical model in order to develop an interpersonal relationship where specially trained play therapists employ the therapeutic capabilities of play to aid clients avoid or overcome problems with their psychosocial lives and to achieve maximum expansion as well as development." Simply put, simple, play therapists employ various play-based instruments and techniques to broaden and improve the process of therapy and to make it more accessible for kids.

In in the 1920s, psychologists realized the importance of play in helping children control their emotions, develop their abilities as well as develop understanding of their own experiences. However, it took another two decades or so before the concepts became established as a method of therapy that was formalized. Since play-based therapies became more formalized and researched the researchers found that the effectiveness of play therapy doesn't come from simply because it's an approach that is more child-friendly in practicing therapy. Instead, they discovered that the core of playing is the healing aspect. Play can aid with developing attachment. development of attachment, which is the connection a child feels with the person they care for. Playing can enhance self-expression, as well as management and control of emotions as well as anxiety. The play also helps build the child's resiliency, increasing their capacity to handle difficulties throughout their life.

Therapists working with children aged 3 to 9 use a type that involves play. Numerous hospitals, schools as well as doctor's offices and mental health clinics have shifted towards recruiting therapists that have worked using play therapy methods.

How Play Therapy Works

The most important elements of therapy for everyone in any stage of life is to be able to feel safe. Involving children in play helps to create the feeling of security and bonding within a therapy setting. If a child feels safe in the hands of a therapist, they will be able to start the various steps of growth and healing through the therapeutic procedure.

Most treatments, which includes play therapy are based on a specific framework of the treatment. This structure starts by establishing the feeling of safety and trust between the therapist and their family. The next step is to develop an action plan for treatment or goals they're trying to reach with the parents and children. It could include identifying emotions and control of impulses as well as anxiety management strategies and processing trauma.

Every session of play therapy is unique, since each is tailored towards satisfying the specific needs of the child at the moment. Certain sessions may involve noisy, messy active play other sessions may be more soft, focussed or slow-paced play. For an uninitiated observer, a therapeutic session may not appear any different than "just playing." In the course of the time, therapists are alert and focused, playing with the child to help the child reach the objectives of therapy. Sometimes, it could be the case that the therapist is engaged in storytelling, role-playing or by using toys with a sand tray or playing what seems as a fun and absurd game. Every interaction has an intention and a purpose within the therapy process.

Play therapy is a mix of methods and theories. The two most widely-respected structures are the nondirective and the directive that are described in the subsequent section. Play therapists often combine abilities as well as tools that are a part of each of these types.

Nondirective Play Therapy

The nondirective approach to play allows the child to play with the language they are used to using to guide the therapy session. The nondirective play therapist set the tone for treatment through allowing children to be in the therapeutic space as they wish. This way children can go on difficulties at their own pace.

Directive Play Therapy

Directive play therapy employs specific intervention based on play that is led by a therapy therapist. This is distinct from nondirective where children lead the sessions. Direct play therapy typically uses commonly-used therapeutic methods like developing coping skills and helps make them more developmental appropriate for children making use of play.

Key Play Therapy Techniques

The following section outlines the most common strategies and methods employed by play therapists. This section's goal isn't to instruct you on the art of being the best play therapist, however, rather, to help you gain the knowledge the nature of play therapy and what it may involve.

Toys and Objects

Play therapists are likely to be able to find toys and other objects accessible. The majority of toys are placed easily accessible open shelves. It allows children to pick the items they require and wants to use.

Metaphors and Storytelling

The use of metaphors and stories to explain a scenario similar to what the child is experiencing while not actually discussing the child. This method allows children to be safe and less enmeshed with their own struggles until they're ready tackle their problems directly. A lot of children employ stories and metaphors naturally and therapists help the child to create or refine the story the child has made up.

Role-Play

It is commonly employed as a method for children to master or to feel confident when faced with a difficult scenario. An excellent example is when preparing for an appointment with a doctor. The child playing the role of a doctor, and the therapist take on the role of a child helps the child to feel confident and in the control of their situation, making to feel prepared and competent at the time of their appointment.

Creative Arts

Drawing, painting and making music, or crafting or other activities--is powerful means of expression, which lots of play therapists utilize.

Imagery and Fantasy

Fantasy and imagery let children utilize their imaginations to tackle difficulties. The counselor might help the child to envision that the daily stress they face is just a tiny worry beast who lives within their head and that they are able to defeat the monster and become the brave knight.

Game Play

Children are able to learn impulse control and turn-taking, as well as emotional regulation and many more social skills by playing games. They are used frequently for learning and practicing new abilities in developmentalally suitable ways.

The Benefits of Play Therapy

Neuroscientist and psychologist Jaak Panksepp has discovered that playing creates areas in the brain required for the regulation of emotions creative thinking, impulse control and many more. Early development creates effects on the brain which persist throughout your life. At the beginning of 2000, scientists at Harvard Medical School found that playing a certain level throughout a person's lifetime could affect the person's emotional and physical health until retirement. It also showed that creativity, generated by play in a younger age is directly related with a person's feeling of health and happiness.

The study of play has found it to significantly improve an individual's executive functioning abilities. They are skills that are required for problem solving, planning as well as a sense of time and many more. Alongside the effects that playing can have on brain function, it helps strengthen the bonds between children with their caregivers. Studies in the field of interpersonal neurobiology studying how our brain and body are affected and formed by relationships have revealed that regularly joyful and jolly interactions between children and their caretaker can enhance the child's capacity to control their mood, control emotions and develop resilience over the course of their lives.

Since play creates an atmosphere of security and bonding that just talking can't. Through play, children can be in control of an issue that is painful and create alternate scenarios and gain control over an issue you felt helpless about. The security and safety that play provides and the distance metaphorically provides a child with the ability to process and explore large, painful emotions.

Here are a few real benefits that children get from playing therapy:

Increased sense of security and connections with other people

Ability to feel and express feelings

A better understanding of and capability to employ strategies for coping

Greater problem-solving creativity

Capacity to understand emotions and physical symptoms

The ability to deal with difficult emotions like anger, anxiety, fear, sadness and stress

Ability to cope with grief and loss

The ability to form healthy and positive relationships

Ability to recover from the effects of trauma

Enhanced capacity to withstand

Improved self-confidence and self-esteem

Chapter 2: Mindfulness Meets Play Therapy

This chapter discusses the many advantages of mindfulness as well as the way you can effect changes in a few simple steps. Integrating mindfulness into your parenting practices could change how you think of your role as a parent. Additionally, increasing your knowledge of mindfulness will enable your child to participate by engaging them in mindful playing.

What Is Mindfulness?

Have you taken the time to breathe in a slow breath, and then tried to take in the present moment that the moment is in? Did you notice your thoughts bouncing around and not getting caught up within them? If yes, to one or both one of the above questions, then you could have practiced mindfulness!

It is a concept that Dr. Amy Saltzman describes mindfulness as being attentive to the purpose of your life in a way that is compassionate and full of curiosity. When you practice mindfulness, you attempt to be at the present moment, and pay attention to the sensations, thoughts and sensations when they happen. Mindfulness is a part of diverse spiritual and religious tradition. Though meditation is by far one of the most popular ways to cultivate mindfulness, it's by no means the only method. We can integrate mindfulness into our everyday life in easy, fun methods.

Studies have shown that teaching kids to experience the world with a sense of mindfulness offers many advantages. It improves focus on self-concept, emotional regulation, the ability to control impulses, and more. With these advantages becoming more known, therapists, teachers and parents are employing mindfulness to help children learn in many diverse fields. Schools are beginning to incorporate these methods even with kids from the age of three to help them develop emotional awareness and skills for coping.

The Seven Pillars of Mindfulness

Jon Kabat Zinn, the scientist who is a pioneer in the field of mindfulness He has identified seven the pillars of mindfulness. These seven pillars stem from his studies in the design of mindfulness-based stress management (MBSR). This MBSR program is a scientifically based exercise in mindfulness that can reduce stress and helps heal, and has been used since the 1970s. MBSR is now used across the globe and has been shown to aid individuals in developing internal resources, coping strategies and reduce stress. The seven pillars of MBSR work in tandem and each one supports the one to create a solid meditation practice.

Nonjudging

The concept of nonjudgment means taking note of what's occurring without becoming lost in our thoughts, opinions and judgements. The brain's capacity to judge is part of our survival instincts. It is a constant process of evaluating every time as whether it is good, negative or neutral. By practicing nonjudgment, we can focus on the present and right now.

Patience

It is essential to be patient when attempting to cultivate mindfulness. You cannot force yourself or others to become more attentive, similar way to how you can't insist on your child eating or go to the bathroom. It is important to be patient with ourselves while we develop this ability.

Beginner's Mind

This principle is something which children are already practicing and are often exposed to. The beginner's mind allows you to look at a situation in a new way, in the same way as if you've not experienced anything like it similar to what children react when trying things in the very first time.

Trust

Another pillar is trust. youngsters often possess naturally however, a lifelong series of life experiences make it difficult for adult to master. This is simply the action of trusting your instincts and trusting in your personal abilities, intuitions and intelligence.

Nonstriving

The act of not trying to strike is an oddity because it's very easy, yet it can be difficult. It is the practice of being nondoing, which is simply inviting yourself to observe the present moment, without any expectations or desire to produce something different than what you're currently enjoying.

Acceptance

Being content with the way things are can't mean a passive resignation. Instead, it's an acceptance of the things as they are right now. If we are able to remain in the present and the better we are able to be aware of how fast things can change. When we are able to combine our the awareness of how fast things can change and our capacity to be able to embrace the changing circumstances We can find peace in this moment.

Letting Go

As we become more mindful and meditation, we will recognize our struggles to let things go. Human nature is to keep track of every moment and be a slave to it. Letting let go of things is essential to be mindful in the present. If we don't fixate too much on an event, we're able to be able to accept it as it actually is.

The Benefits of Mindfulness

The benefits of mindfulness can be benefited by anyone at any stage of life, ranging from kids to seniors. The most beneficial aspect of mindfulness is the ability to use the techniques to a wide range of scenarios. In my case, for instance I was teaching an evening mindfulness class for an elementary school group. A few days later, I got a text message from my classroom instructor about how this class of students were using mindfulness. One student was angry and during the emotional turmoil Two other students impulsively came up to the student and reminded him of the power of his breath. The group worked together to aid the child in distress to find his breath, and then return to a state of calm. They had developed the capacity to apply the practices of mindfulness beyond the school setting, and apply these skills at the moment! Mindfulness provided them with practical skills for helping a troubled friend deal with his emotional issues.

There are other advantages from practicing mindfulness:

Reduces negative self-talk

Increases one's self-compassion

Limits the negative effects of stress

Reduces the force on the frequency and intensity of rumination or obsessive thinking.

Reduces depression and anxiety.

Increases the ability to recognize an individual's feelings

Increases the ability to manage emotions, control, and regulate emotions

Enhances awareness of the present moment.

Increases the sleep quality sleep

Increases compassion towards others

After you have a better understanding of the meaning behind play therapy and the advantages that mindfulness can bring, we'll see ways that the two complement one another.

Using Mindfulness in Play and Play Therapy

Mindfulness-based play includes engaging in a variety of fun and exciting exercises that educate both kids and adults how to remain focused on the present. For caregivers and parents, mindfulness exercises can help them be aware of their own emotions as well as their reactions to stressful situations. This will allow for more effective relationships between them and their child.

In a therapeutic setting the play therapists utilize techniques based on mindfulness to train the child on specific techniques through play, using the seven principles of mindfulness. Play therapy that has an emphasis on mindfulness children can conquer numerous challenges in life through enhancing their awareness and expression of emotion as well as establishing an optimistic self-concept (their perception of their own self) and enhancing impulse control as well as developing self-calming abilities. An experienced therapist for mindful play together with mindfulness-focused activities will create an effective path towards healing and progress.

It is vital to make the differences between play therapy that has an emphasis on mindfulness and games that are based on play in the book. The activities aim to assist you in engaging and play with children in a fun manner using the lens of mindfulness. Though some of the exercises have similarities to what which a play therapy therapist could be able to engage children to engage in during a therapeutic play session, these activities have been modified to make them suitable to the nature of play that occurs between parents/caregiver and child within a home environment.

The benefits from Play Therapy with a Mindfulness focus

If a child is upset or sad, or is not paying attention, it may create difficult emotions for parents. At these times parents may experience memories of their memories of childhood, or even recalling their anger and shame the child felt. If this occurs, they might lose their ability remain present for the child they love and provide their child with a sense of security by their quiet and grounded presence. Parents and caregivers may employ techniques of mindfulness to develop an awareness of the present moment and gain insight. The more mindful we are of our personal emotional reactions and triggers, based on the experiences we have had in our lives and experiences, the more attentive and present in our relationship with children's needs.

Playing using a mindful focus give the possibility of connecting to our present experience and our personal experiences as well as our children's as well, it provides an environment that is suitable to teach children this ability, especially since mindfulness cannot be taught in a formal manner. If children are able to play in the practice of mindfulness using a game-based manner, they're better able to apply the technique in everyday activities. Furthermore, if parents are attentive and conscious of their own emotions it is more likely help their child achieve tranquility in the moment. If you as a parent stay calm and relaxed during the child's emotional turmoil it automatically opens up the foundation for calming to be able to follow. If the child and you are engaged in activities with mindfulness attention, the greater chance you'll be able to get grounded and calm during difficult times.

From Playing to Prospering: A Play Therapy Success Story

Play therapy and mindfulness could result in an incredibly positive transformation. The client I work with Julie (confidential details have been changed to protect her confidentiality reasons) began therapy at age eight as she struggled with the divorce of her parents. Mom observed that Julie felt overwhelmed by her emotions, and she didn't know how to let them out, sometimes becoming violent at her siblings and mother.

Julie started her treatment by taking part in play therapy sessions every week. Through the course of therapy, Julie worked on expressing her feelings and coping with the effects of divorce from her parents. Alongside receiving the therapeutic benefits of play-based therapy for children, Julie learned coping skills via games played with an eye on mindfulness. She was able to observe her emotions in the moment and deciding safe and healthy methods to express herself. Julie's mother noticed she was beginning using the techniques she was taught in therapy for example, naming what she felt in that moment, focusing on emotions, and using healthy methods to communicate emotions. In time, Julie no longer required weekly therapy sessions, and she was assured of her ability to be aware of her feelings and manage the emotions with a sense of calm!

Positive Outcomes for You and Your Child

The practice of mindfulness with play therapy focused on the present can bring about positive results for children and adults when it is used frequently and regularly. The potential advantages of mindfulness to parents/caregivers as well as children are:

Parent/Caregiver-Child Connection: Helps develop a strong connection, the first step in creating any behavior change in your child.

Emotional Expression and Regulation It allows both you and your child to understand and voice your feelings. The ability to better regulate or manage your reactions and emotions can help you be the soothing the child's needs in times of high emotional turmoil.

Learning to Ground and Cope Skills Like coping abilities grounded skills help let you be present in the moment, and not simply finding peace. Regulated does not always mean peaceful however, it's more about our capacity to control our emotions during the moment. Skills for grounding help us stay at the moment long sufficient to implement strategies to cope.

Mind Body Connection: It helps both you and your child develop more awareness of how the body and mind work with each other in this moment.

The management of stress and anxiety Enhances the capacity to handle and cope with anxiety and stress.

The present moment is focusing upon our present experience at the present moment. When we are in the present moment there is no thought of the past, or future. We are only focusing on the present moment.

The concept of focus and attention is the capacity to be attentive only one thing, activity or job at a time. Attention is the ability to pay attention to the presence of something or someone.

Self-Compassion and Confidence: Aids improve self-compassion. It helps cultivate self-love, self-confidence, and ability to endure difficult situations.

Creativity and flexible thinking The term "creativity" refers to the capacity to think outside the box as well as develop innovative concepts. Flexible thinking refers to the ability to see things differently. It is helpful in adjusting to sudden changes, or in resolving the issue of a change.

The Executive Functioning Skill: Enhances capability to control time as well as order details and follow instructions.

Impulse Control: Provides children with the opportunity to have fun while practicing dealing with impulsive behavior, and reduce conflict.

Relaxation and Calm: Enhances the child's capacity to sleep and remain in bed, leading to peaceful nights and happy days.

Chapter 3: Tools & Tips For Mindful Play

In this chapter, you will discover how you can get maximum value from the book. It will provide you with useful tools and strategies for establishing an enjoyable and positive experience with mindfulness. Even though you're not experienced in having fun with your child The following information will make you to feel more comfortable when you begin your activities.

Listen and Let Your Child Lead

As parents and caretakers, we forget the little influence children are in. A large portion of our child's life is controlled by others. However, children must experience the feeling of control, power and the ability to control. This creates a feeling of security and are crucial for development. When children exhibit problematic behaviors, it's due to the fact that they feel unobserved and feel like they are in no power.

Mindfulness-based play can be a fantastic approach to build an experience where your child is in control and feel empowered. If you are able to engage with your children in this form of game, your goal is to create a sense of connection and build a sense of shared or equal influence. As a parent or caregiver it is your job to embody the principles that are a part of mindful (discussed in chapter 2.) to facilitate this kind of connection. Your child will gain not only from being able to take control of the present as well as the feeling of being seen and heard by the person you are.

In order to create this sense of connection and presence, just enjoy your child's play by letting them take the lead and lead the action. Do not be tempted to do multiple tasks such as taking care of the dishes or checking emails while playing. Be present with your child in those moments. What is this like? This could mean playing on the ground and your child playing at eyes level, or following them in their direction with no judgment or expectations. If you are tempted to alter or change the game to something else that what your child is making, stop. Breathe deeply and think about the importance of your child experiencing the feeling that they are in control. You should try to communicate the things they're doing at the moment as if you were an announcer for a sporting event. The conversation could be something similar to "Oh I know how to deal with it! Then you're going to put it out on the table. Fantastic move!" Being with your child in this manner enhances the sense of seeing and increases their relationship with your.

Creating a Safe and Playful Space

The practice of mindfulness can be played almost everywhere with little or any materials. This is because the type of play has its roots in your relationship to your kid. Whatever the size of the play area, or the lack of it the play space will be the right size! The thing that makes the playground perfect is the passion and enthusiasm you apply to your activities when you play alongside your child. It's all about the simplicity in having your child play using a mindful approach. Play spaces don't require expensive toys or other objects. Common household items, simple toys and the basics of arts and crafts will be all that is required outside of the relationship and your children.

As a parent/caregiver have the power and capability to help your child feel emotional and physically safe as well as being noticed and respected during any event. If you're present and connected to your children, the better they'll be.

Alongside the presence and connectivity There are additional strategies that you can employ to make your play enjoyable safe and fun. A good way to do this is by setting the boundaries of playing. While you are playing with your child, and take their direction however, it's important to ensure they are safe within the boundaries of your house. If you're not happy having your child jump on the sofa or running through the home, for instance but you still need to establish the boundaries. An easy and effective method to accomplish this is to tell your child "I realize you're begging me to chase after you throughout the home. At home it is our walking feet. I could chase you with my feet, or using my creeping feet instead." This puts limits while offering the child an option and yet allowing them to engage with playing.

Another approach could be utilized when a child is struggling in letting go of the activity. Making time for play with parents or caregivers can be a lot of fun for children which can be difficult to leave. If your child tends to be upset or throw fights when time is up, think about the use of a digital timer to guide your child's playtime. Your child should set the timer before the time for play; this will give them an understanding of their situation and an understanding of the length of time is going to last. Keep in mind that you remain being the caretaker/parent. The way your child is led by you doesn't mean throwing every rule out of your door!

How to Make the Most of This Book

The games included in the book were developed with kids ranging from the age of three to nine years old in their minds. As a parent or a caregiver who is the best of your child. As you work through the exercises, you should use your discretion to pick activities that you feel are appropriate to your child's needs, regardless of age. Each of the activities within the book are performed in a separate way and you are at ease to move from chapter to chapter in order to discover the one that is well for you and your child at the present.

The 80 games and activities are split up into six chapters. In the beginning, activities focus on breath, the body, as well as movement. The final chapter provides exercises for mindfulness which can be done outdoors. Each page of activities outlines how long the game will last and the potential advantages, as well as any materials necessary (if there are any) along with step-by-step instruction. The majority of the games offer suggestions for modifications or other ideas to help make your playtime more conscious.

One of my most favorite games is known as "Notice Mind". It teaches children a fun song to help your child to get ready for go out of the home. Every parent I've had the pleasure of meeting would say that getting children prepared, dressed and on their way to the airport is stressful. It's a quick and fun method to increase awareness, and possibly transform the stress to a more positive experience.

Activity Quick Reference

Utilize this table to assist find activities that will help strengthen certain abilities. Each exercise is classified by the area they can aid in.

Potential Benefits Activities

Parent/Caregiver-Child Connection Together Breaths

Stuffy Talks

Mindful Hockey

Back Art

Notice Mind

Emotional Expression & Regulation Butterfly Hug

Power Pose

Jumping Feelings Scale

Feelings Song

Weather Report

The Feelings Wave

Grounding & Coping Skills Mirror Breath

Breathing Times

Sunshine and Snow Clouds

Barefoot Breathing

Mind-Body Connection Iceberg Rescue

Body Check

Human GPS

Music Mind

Mindfulness Hike

Stress & Anxiety Management Lumberjacks

I Am a Tree

My Favorite Color

Magic Carpet Ride

Feel My Feelings

Worry Bug

Present-Moment Awareness Taste Experiment

Puppy Mind

Word Focus

Mud Pie Magic

Mindful Walking Path

Focus & Attention Ring-a-Ding-Ding

Music Hide-and-Seek

Focused Tree

Artistic Focus

Freeze Wand

Self-Compassion & Confidence Hugging the World

Animal Sidekick

Mantra Stone

I Am Unique

Kindness Bands

Creativity & Flexible Thinking Artist Eyes

Movie Magic

Imagine a World

Pass the Story

Scribble Thoughts

Trash Mind

Executive Functioning Skills Mountain Wiggle

Space Explorer

Movie Magic

Morning Hunt

Camera Eyes

Impulse Control Slow-Motion Moves

Personal Space Bubble

Mindfulness Jar

Focused Tree

Wiggle, Jump, Freeze, Walk

Calm & Relaxation Body Scan, Body Layers

Push It

Ceiling Watch

Sound Vibrations

Breathing in Color

Chapter 4: Body, Breath, & Movement

One of the most effective methods to develop mindfulness is to connect with our breath, bodies and movements. In this chapter, you'll explore fun and engaging movement exercises to teach your child to be aware of their body present. Then, you'll move your body using a conscious approach to increase self-confidence as well as the ability to regulate emotions. Your child will discover the different ways they can find strength in their breathing. The breath is our most powerful tools which can alter or change completely the way we react to any circumstance immediately. The activities that conclude this section provide fun ways for you as well as your child to build an even stronger connection by engaging in exercises that demand concentration. The more conscious we are of our body and how they move, the more controlled in our movements, grounded, and compassionate to ourselves and others we develop.

Together Breaths

3 to 5 minutes

If your child is upset angered, agitated, or the midst of an argument Your presence of calm could suffice to assist them achieve peace. The simple but effective breathing practice encourages the child and you to work on breathing together. Try this exercise in moments of peace so that you are able to apply it whenever big emotions appear.

BENEFITS: Emotional Expression & Regulation, Parent/Caregiver-Child Connection, Grounding & Coping Skills

1. Begin in a relaxed seated place, with yourself and the kid looking at one another. You should be in a position where your knees meet.

2. After that, place your hands over the child's heart, and ask your child to place their hands on your heart.

3. Together Take a deep breath in, breathing extremely slowly through the nose for the

count of three. Then, breath out with the mouth until you reach five.

4. Be aware of the way that breaths are flowing through and out of the other's bodies. Examine if you and the child can match your breathing patterns.

5. Begin to notice each your heartbeats changing with every breath.

6. Take as many deep breaths as you can in a moment that feels comfortable.

Continue to play Do not be afraid to change your seating position. Children may like to sit back-to-back, or be in your lap snugly tucked in while you breath together, trying to mimic the rhythm of each other.

Slow-Motion Moves

5-10 mins

It can aid your child to explore and observe physical sensations. The pace of life is fast and it is difficult to take the time to slow down enough often to truly notice how our bodies experience. The game of slow motion together with your child is an excellent way to let children begin to notice the connections to their bodies and the current moment.

BENEFITS: Mind-Body Connection, Present-Moment Awareness, Self-Compassion & Confidence, Impulse Control

Material: Any kind of music

1. Introduce to your child that you'll be attempting to move your body at different speeds. Then take note of the way your body is feeling at the moment.

2. Discuss with your child the kind of body movement you would like to perform for example, dancing, shaking or wiggle or make ninja-like moves. Be imaginative!

3. Select music that both of you each enjoy dancing to. When you move around, make sure to observe what your body is experiencing. Make a list of the things you observe as you move, then ask your child to

follow suit. Like, for instance, are your legs burning or hot? Are your eyes sweaty?

4. Then, pick a slower music that you are able to perform your body movements in slow-motion. Do the same moves to those you've done prior to. Consider how different it feels when you move this method. Make a list of your observations, then encourage your child to follow exactly the same.

MASTER MINDFULNESS TIP: Tell your child to to link their breath to every move. As they integrate their breath into their movements, they will gain the awareness they'll develop.

Body Scan

5-10 mins

Through this exercise, you are able to help your child observe the body's parts one at one time. When they are moving through every part of the body they may begin to feel the sensations they are experiencing in this instant. As your child becomes capable of connecting to their body, the more easy it is easier for them to recognize and articulate what they want.

BENEFITS: Mind-Body Connection, Emotional Expression & Regulation, Calm & Relaxation

1. Find a cozy spot within your home to allow your child to lay down.

2. Tell your child to shut their eyes, or gaze down towards the floor. Ask them to pay attention to their breathing as they breathe into and out. It is suggested that they observe the belly of their child moving upwards and downwards with every breath. Stop for a moment to give the child time to observe the rhythm of their breathing.

3. Tell them to look at the soles of their feet. Check to see if they sense all the way into their toes and feet. Check if they sense their entire foot. Pause briefly.

4. Then, they should move your leg. Examine if they are able to feel the ankles, knees as well as the entire leg. Do they feel hot or

cold? Are they tired or overflowing with enthusiasm? Pause briefly.

5. Moving on toward the belly. Check with your child to see if you observe their belly moving between up and down each breath. Pause briefly.

6. Then move on to your shoulder and arms. Do they feel stiff and firm like raw spaghetti, or loose and wiggly, like cooked spaghetti? Check to see if you can feel their fingertips. Do they feel cold or hot? Do they seem agitated or is it still? Pause again.

7. Start to pay attention to their nose, mouth, eyes and even on top of their heads. Also, make sure they observe their entire body all the way from their toes up and up to the top of their heads. Encourage them to take a long breath and exhale as they gently wiggle your fingers and toes. And lastly, ask that they should slowly close their eyes.

8. When your child is done with your body scan you can talk about the things that were

easy and difficult to notice different aspects of their bodies.

MASTER MINDFULNESS TIPS The following is a fantastic idea to practice right before going to bed. A body scan will aid your child to relax and grounded.

Butterfly Hug

3 to 5 minutes

It is recommended to instruct to practice calm breathing and moves while your child is at peace. These instruments during an angry or agitated moment, but this isn't the time to start practicing the techniques! Utilizing mindful tools to calm yourself can help them improve their abilities and allow you to make use of them in difficult times. The butterfly hug helps relax the body by using the breath and the nervous system. The first time it was used was by Lucina Artigas at the start of the 90s to aid survivors of the hurricane Pauline at Acapulco, Mexico.

BENEFITS: Emotional Expression & Regulation, Grounding & Coping Skills, Calm & Relaxation, Stress & Anxiety Management

1. Let your child place the arms across their chests with their hands resting just under their shoulders. If this feels good it is, they may interlock their thumbs to create an image of butterflies.

2. Then, instruct them to take a long complete breath in through their noses and out via the mouth.

3. When they take a deep breath and slowly, they should begin gently tapping the chest with their hands with their hands lifted and returning them to their original position in a manner as if they were wings of a butterfly.

4. Do this with your child until the time it is comfortable for them, and they work hard to pay attention to their breath.

Continue to play: Develop your connection with your child through telling them the things you admire about them while they offer them a kiss. Talk about a moment in the past where you felt happy with them or something they accomplished that caused you to smile. If you are happy with your child, it strengthens the bond between you and, in turn, increase your child's behaviour and self-esteem.

Personal Space Bubble

For 3-5 minutes

This activity's goal is to aid your child discover how to recognize their body's boundaries. Establishing a relationship with our bodies, and knowing the factors that make us feel safe as well as unsafe can be an effective tool! In this exercise we will discuss the way you feel to be the one in charge of your body and the extent to which your individual space is comfortable for you.

BENEFITS: Impulse Control, Mind-Body Connection, Self-Compassion & Confidence

1. Tell your child they'll be participating in an activity where they have to determine how

much of their private space they will need in order to make their bodies feel safe.

2. Then, you must decide whom will be your body's boss, and who will be the person who invades the body.

3. From the opposite side of the room an intruder is advancing towards the body boss slow and in a quiet manner.

4. A body boss will raise his hand in a signal to stop whenever they sense that the intruder gets too close. If the person who is intruding notices that the body boss is raising their hand, they is required to freeze in place the place they're.

5. Switch roles now, where the intruder becomes the body boss, and the body boss turning into the intruder.

Master Mindfulness Tips The following is an excellent method to educate your child about the autonomy of their bodies and a notion that can aid your child all through their entire life. It is also a great opportunity to discuss others in your child's life that might allow them to become closer or far from their private area.

Lumberjacks

The time is 3-5 minutes

At times, we are sluggish. Perhaps we've had a tiring morning at work, or your child was waking up with no energy. This exercise is a fantastic opportunity to reenergize yourself even if you're feeling lower than 100 percent. Be aware of how your sensations shift with this fun, simple move is an effective opportunity to develop your awareness.

BENEFITS: Emotional Expression & Regulation, Mind-Body Connection, Stress & Anxiety Management

1. Provide your child with the following directions:

It is. Assume you're living in a forest and you see high trees in the distance. The tree you cut down was massive tree, and you intend to cut it up into smaller bits of wood.

b. You're so strong that you take down that huge tree! Be strong and tall. (Have your child place their feet just a bit larger than the hip distance.)

C. Imagine in the grip of an axe. Secure your fingers by wrapping your one hand between the wrists of your opposite hand. Inhale deeply and then raise your hands above your head.

D. Imagine yourself hitting your ax hard to cut wood!

It is. Breathe deeply while letting your arms fall towards the floor. Relax your body and let your hands move through your legs.

2. If you're feeling inclined, complete things alongside your kid.

3. Repeat as often as you'd like!

Master Mindfulness Tip: Have your child connect their breath to their movements.

Then observe how they feel. Check with them to see if their body sensations are different or identical.

Mountain Wiggle

3 to 5 minutes

The focus of this activity is to build the ability to concentrate through physical connection. Both of you and your child will work together to squeeze the body part at one time. Though it might sound simple however, it takes concentration and precision to be able to have fun with only a portion of your body!

BENEFITS: Impulse Control, Mind-Body Connection, Focus & Attention, Executive Functioning Skills

1. Your child should stand up on their side. Make sure your child is aware of keeping their body safe regardless of the fact that you're about having fun.

2. Start wiggling your bodies. Encourage your child to pay attention only the feet. Let them

just wiggle their toes and then move around on their feet.

3. Have your child notice the legs of their children. Make them wiggle their legs at first slowly and then move them super fast. Moving to different parts within the human body. Watch your child observe and then wiggle their hips shoulders, arms, hands and heads.

4. Then, let your child dance their entire body simultaneously. Allow them to wiggle for 10 to 15 minutes. Do the same with your child! Your child can return to stillness by counting the number of seconds, and telling them, "We will move until I reach one. Find a still-body in three minutes, locate the still body within two. Find an unmoving body!

5. As soon as you've both become an unmoving body and you both take an exhale and breathe in.

MASTER MINDFULNESS TIP: Try playing the game reversed for a more challenging experience. Begin by wiggle your entire body. Stop wiggling just one part of your body at one time and continue until you remain still. This process requires greater concentration and focus.

Mirror Breath 5-10 minutes

Mirror breath is an easy and enjoyable way to teach deep breathing. Research discovered to be the calmest kind of breathing that we perform. To deepen our breathing you exhale more than we breathe in. The body is signaling that it's safe and can relax, this is crucial to calm.

BENEFITS: Stress & Anxiety Management, Focus & Attention, Grounding & Coping Skills, Emotional Expression & Regulation

Materials: Mirrors windows, mirrors, or another reflective surfaces

1. Locate a window or mirror at home where allows your child to get close enough where they are able to almost kiss the glass.

2. Ask your child to breathe through their noses until they reach a number of.

3. Let your child breathe out while their mouth is open towards the window or mirror. Encourage them to exhale in a long, hard breath so that they don't get the glass! Make sure they breathe for a minimum of four (or greater, if it is possible).

4. Repeat the process a couple of times. Let your child's eyes get clogged up mirror for as long as it is it is.

Keep playing: Encourage your child to draw a few drawings to the hazy surface by writing messages such as I love you or a positive affirmation such as I'm strong, or faces of emotion.

Power Pose

10 to 15 minutes

The nervous system of our body plays a important role in the regulation of our mood. In the event of a stressful or traumatizing moment, our nervous system is able to store information relating to the experience. That's how the body's structure has changed through time in order to make sure we're safe. However, the knowledge stored in our bodies may cause us to respond to a negative response or in an unnatural way to an event which we believe to be like the last challenging or traumatizing incident, even if it's not. The process can aid in helping the body regulate and manage our feelings in the current time without overreacting.

BENEFITS: Emotional Expression & Regulation, Mind-Body Connection, Self-Compassion & Confidence

1. Have your child imagine an experience or occasion they would like to be successful, such as the first time they dance or riding their bike.

2. Together, determine how you and your child will be during the occasion, for example, confident peaceful, serene, or powerful.

3. Have your child display to you their body how they appear like when they feel like this. It might be holding hands to their hips, or reaching upwards to the sky. However you pose your body will be appropriate! The position they choose will determine their power point.

4. Then, have them contemplate the opposite experience and then pose. The body could be rolled into a ball or shoulders may be in a slump, and the head downwards. This is a pose that they call the Stuck Body.

5. Then, have your child begin with their body in a stuck pose and observe what it is like to be in this posture. If they're at ease, let them shift into their power posture!

6. When they take their power pose, let your child think about what they would like to achieve. Encourage them to describe how they would like to feel by using an empowering "I" phrase, such as, I'm courageous! or I can do it!

7. You can repeat this game for as many times as your child wants. You must ensure that they speak their statement of power loudly when they are done.

Master Mindfulness Tip: Extend the exercise by imitating the movements your child is making and speaking. Repeat the motions in the same way while they transition from their standing to power poses. Repetition their statement of power and encourage them to repeat the statement in a loud and loud voice. If you want to make it even more enjoyable, have your child lie on their beds while they repeat the phrase. If you notice that your child's body is huge and tall, it will increase the pleasure within their body.

Mindful Jungle Exploration

15-20 minutes

As part of this program participants will practice active mindfulness through the creation of an imaginary landscape within your own home. Active mindfulness involves taking note of how the body reacts to us when we breathe and move. Explore mindfulness in a fun way with the joy of movement, imagination as well as focusing on your breath!

BENEFITS: Focus & Attention, Present-Moment Awareness, Mind-Body Connection

Materials: Pillows, blankets, stuffed animals laundry baskets, chairs

1. Utilize the materials suggested or any other materials you may have at the shelf to make an imagined pathway through your backyard.

2. Then, guide your child through the following steps:

a. Take a deep breath in.

b. Take note of each area of your body. Give some wiggle. Begin with your feet. Then, wiggle your legs shoulders, belly, hands as well as shoulders. Finally, head.

C. Allow your focus to extend to the entire body. You are now eager to discover!

3. Have your child move slow and quietly along the path of jungle with their conscious body. Help them by asking questions like: how do your feet feel? What do you feel moving your arms and legs?

4. It is important to remind them that when their minds wander then they need to return it to the present moment by keeping their eyes on the ground.

5. Take your child on a walk along the path through the woods a couple of times. Every time striving to remain focused on their body.

Continue to play: Be your own fun. The child could pretend to be various jungle animals by crawling, slithering in a trance, jumping or running across the field. The more sluggish the movements and the less difficult it is to focus on a single part of your body.

Hugging the World

5-10 mins

The aim of this game is to encourage your child to practise giving love and affection to those around them. Love is the cornerstone of meditation. Studies show that the more that we cultivate loving-kindness more, we are happier.

BENEFITS: Self-Compassion & Confidence, Grounding & Coping Skills

Materials: Colored and paper materials (optional)

1. Ask your child to imagine all the world around them or draw the world on paper. Discuss the places that your child's been to at, for example, the park, school, or maybe even a location in the distance your family could be going to.

2. Have your child imagine places in the world that they've never visited but would love to see if they could visit - perhaps Disney World, Africa, or even the North Pole!

3. Your child can imagine sending love, positive thoughts to all and every thing on the planet employing the following words:

a. Imagine you're offering the entire world a large hug. It's so huge that it covers the places that you visit everyday, places like schools, as well as places that you aren't.

b. Breathe deeply. Spread your arms and lift them out wide, large enough to squeeze the entire world within.

C. Then exhale, and then send your most sweet heartfelt, loving, and kind thoughts to all of the world!

4. Repeat the process multiple times.

Keep playing: After your child is done with the activity, ask them to continue drawing images of their world, filled by their kindness and love. Encourage them to think about what the world could appear like if just filled with loving and caring.

Breathing Times

3.0 - 3.5 minutes

The breath we take is among the most effective tools for mindfulness. Find ways to playfully engage in mindful breathing activities with your youngsters will improve their capacity to utilize their breath as a source of energy for difficult situations. This activity are using a clock to determine the number of breaths your child and you are able to complete in a minute!

BENEFITS: Grounding & Coping Skills, Calm & Relaxation, Emotional Expression & Regulation

Material: Any timer of any sort

1. Decide if you would like to try breath at a slower pace (inhaling for three, exhaling five times) or even breathe (inhaling for four, exhaling after four).

2. Then, decide on a duration of time that is suitable to you and your child. This can be as short as one minute, two minutes or even thirty seconds.

3. Begin the timer, and then try to see how many or few breaths your child and you are able to take! Make sure you keep track of it by holding one finger in every time you take a breath.

4. Make sure your child remembers to breathe through their nasal passage and then exhale out of the mouth.

Master Mindfulness Tips: Let your child focus exclusively on the feelings of their breath. Not the time of the clock. What does air feel like when it enters their nostrils is it different when it exits the mouth? Take note of the sensations of their lungs when they're inhaling air. The more physical sensations your child is aware of and experiences, the more at peace.

Heart and Body Dance

10 to 15 minutes

The process of connecting to our bodies is difficult for children as well as adults. The way to improve this connection is through exaggerated experiences that are centered on the body. One fun and easy method to create this experience with your child is by turning on some tunes and dance around.

BENEFITS: Mind-Body Connection, Emotional Expression & Regulation

MATERIALS: Music

1. As a family, you can choose the songs you would like to play.

2. Let your child look around their body prior to when you start. Try saying"Let's be aware of how we feel before starting. Request them to pay the heartbeat of their body and observe if it's quick or slowly.

3. Play the music, and begin dancing. Your goal is to dance with enough energy to alter the rhythm of your heart.

4. After about a minute after a couple of minutes, stop the music and cease the dancing.

5. Request your child to sit still and breathe the deep breath while you breathe in through the nose, and then out with the mouth.

6. Your child should look around their body like in step 2. Focus their attention on the rhythm of their heart. Find out if the heart beats quicker or slower.

7. Continue to dance for several additional minutes, and then have your child listen to the heartbeat of their child again. Check to see if it's similar to earlier or is it different.

Keep playing: Choose an instrumental that is quiet and slow and move your body slower, moving your body more slowly, or wiggling with slow speed. After a couple of minutes stop the music, and ask your child to check the heart rate. Find out what the effect of dancing to slow music can alter their heart rate.

Animal Moves

15-20 minutes

The activity involves simple yoga postures that are common to all as an enjoyable way of experiencing mindfulness in movements. If we try unfamiliar or difficult moves, we transmit our bodies a message that we're healthy. When the body responds that way, it could boost our self-confidence.

BENEFITS: Self-Compassion & Confidence, Mind-Body Connection, Parent/Caregiver-Child Connection

Mats: Yoga mat or a mat for exercise (optional)

1. Sing this song (to the melody from "The Farmer and the Dell") while you and your child move their body parts:

Hold my hands in the air, (stand with feet shoulder distance apart, arms reaching towards the sky)

Drop them to the bottom, (fold forward at the hips, with arms open)

Restore them toward the ceiling, Mountain Pose. (return to standing on hands above your head)

2. Make it more challenging by adding music and movement:

Retrace my steps at a nice, slow pace. This can be called Plank Pose. (do an incline plank, resting your feet on the floor If you need to)

Bring your belly to the floor It's time to become snake. you'll have fun being a snake. (lie your stomach on the floor and put your hands on the shoulders and gentle lifting the neck and head)

Aim your hips towards the sky. it's time to become a dog. Woof, woof, woof. It's good to be a puppy. (press down on your hands while lifting the hips upwards and keep your feet planted to the ground)

Chapter 5: Sensory Awareness

Reconnecting our body and mind through mindful practice can have many advantages. All of our experiences and feelings are stored as energy within our bodies. In many instances the body reacts to an event with a specific way, before we even know that we're reacting. In spite of this connection we often ignore the body-mind connection. At a very young age the children are usually trained to disregard the emotions that are present in their body. As this goes on more often, the less capable to perceive the sensations in their bodies as valuable information or clues in knowing what they want. It helps to help your child re-learn and strengthen this crucial ability to live life! This chapter's activities give you a fun way to encourage your child to discover this subject by creating an awareness of their five senses- being able to feel, hearing the sensation of smelling, tasting, and looking.

Body Layers

For a period of 3-5 minutes

This is an easy method for children to enhance their understanding of the physical feelings. Through visualizing various levels of their bodies and body, they learn to become fully present with their bodies at the moment. This is an excellent method of calming the mind by paying attention.

BENEFITS: Mind-Body Connection, Focus & Attention, Calm & Relaxation

1. Choose a comfy spot where your child can lay or sit. It could be their sofa, bed or the flooring.

2. Help your child take some deep, long breaths. The child may choose to turn their eyes away or gaze towards the ground.

3. When your child is at the right age to go through their body, by reading the following instructions with a calm, slow voice:

a. Take note of a sensation or feeling at the surface that surrounds your body. It could be something you observe taking place to the skin. (pause briefly)

b. Then try to sense the sensation of feeling or a sensation in your body. perhaps underneath the skin. (pause briefly)

C. Check if you feel a certain sensation or a feeling that is deeper within your body. It could be within your head, tummy or even your the heart. (pause briefly)

d. On your next breath in, open your eyes.

4. Ask your child to share the feelings and sensations they experienced in the various parts of their body.

Master Mindfulness Tips for younger kids you can ask them to talk the things they have noticed at the end of each layer, prior to moving onto the next. This is an excellent game to play prior to going to bed, or when you have a job that requires lots of attention for example, homework.

Space Explorer

5-10 mins

Within the seven pillars that comprise mindfulness, the first step is practicing seeing all things through fresh eyes. This is an excellent method to assist your child improve their mindfulness by actively taking note of the world around them.

BENEFITS: Focus & Attention, Executive Functioning Skills

1. Pick a room or a space within your home where your child could pretend is an alien world they've discovered.

2. Ask your child to walk into the space like you've never visited previously.

3. While your child is exploring this brand new "planet," ask them if they see anything that's different, is different, or perhaps you've never seen it previously.

4. Your child should continue to discover and observe changes happening around the

planet, or even move to different planets (rooms) inside your home.

Continue to play In the event that your child has difficulty to be aware of things, you can create evident changes to the environment prior to beginning the exercise. Make a rotation, with your child changing the "planet" before the task is to find out what's changed.

Jumping Feelings Scale

10 to 15 minutes

Recognizing our feelings is the initial step towards knowing how to stay in touch in our experiences. As we become more aware of the emotions we feel as well, the more capable of knowing how to handle them to them in a healthy manner. This exercise uses a visual scale to show the intensity of your feelings for helping build awareness and acceptance in a fun manner.

BENEFITS: Emotional Expression & Regulation, Grounding & Coping Skills, Stress & Anxiety Management

Materials: Writing supplies Ten pieces of paper, animal stuffed toys and books (optional)

1. Begin by drawing the scale of 1 to 10, and then create a scale from 1 to. Write each number on an individual piece of paper, and then line them up on the floor or even line up 10 books or toys for the scale.

2. Your child should be taught by using the script below to explain that the scale is the magnitude of feelings that can occur:

a. At times, emotions seem minor as if they're only a single. They're not a problem for us but they're not dominating. Perhaps there was an time that you were angry, however, you were able to continue whatever you were doing and you didn't require assistance with the anger.

b. Sometimes emotions seem huge, as a 10. It's possible that we need assistance in managing an emotion like that. You must put our thoughts aside and "be" in the moment!

C. Sometimes, feelings fall somewhere between two, such as five. They're not small however they're not massive either. It's possible to "be" by feeling to get some help then continue.

3. Create an inventory of feelings. The list could include anxious, happy, sad and anxious, nervous, scared, or angry, just to mention several.

4. With your child, remember different times when both of you felt all of those emotions. In each emotion experience determine the size of your feeling was on the scale of numbers.

5. Inspire your child to move their body around the scale, whether by leaping at, skipping, running or strolling slow. Choose only movements which feel safe as well as appropriate for the space you live in.

6. If you notice different emotions in your child, don't try to change your child's behavior or actions. It is important for your child to be aware of their emotions and the extent to which they affect them. It helps build emotional acceptance and tolerance.

Master Mindfulness Tips If you are a parent or caretaker It is acceptable for you to openly discuss your honest and appropriate feelings with your child. As an example, you could declare, "I was angered today after my purchase arrived and I was not able to find certain items. The anger I felt was like five. The more we show empathy and understanding and acceptance, the easier these abilities become to our kids.

Taste Experiment

5-10 mins

Mindful eating helps us learn to take a moment and be aware of the food we put within our mouths and engages the senses of taste the smell and. Most of the time, we hurry to eat or stare at screens while eating. It is often a bit jarring and difficult to slow the pace of eating, which makes it an active practice. The mindfulness eating practice alters a traditional mindfulness exercise in order to make it more suitable for young children.

BENEFITS: Focus & Attention, Present-Moment Awareness

MATERIALS: Snack food

1. Choose a snack that you're confident eating with your child during mealtimes. The food should be small enough that they can hold within their mouths for just some time, such as Goldfish crunchers, raisins or M&M's.

2. Tell your child they're planning to conduct a thrilling experiment. Make sure they have a comfortable place to sit and then close their eyes.

3. Listen to the script below in a soft, calm tone of voice:

a. Relax, take a breath into your nostrils and out through your mouth. Be aware of how your body experiencing. Is your stomach feeling hungry? Does your mouth feel dry? (pause briefly)

b. Open your hands. I'm putting a tiny snack inside your hand. Pay attention to the way it is feeling. Do you feel rough? Does it feel soft? Do you think it's soft or rough? (pause briefly)

It is a. Then I'm taking the food beneath your nose. Be attentive to the smell of the food. Do you notice if it is sweet or salty? If you are smelling it, does it make your stomach rumble or making it making your mouth water? (pause briefly)

D. Then, open your mouth and extend your tongue. I'm going to put the snacks into your mouth. Do not chew it immediately! Let it rest upon your tongue. What is the sensation it makes to your tongue? What is the flavor? Salty or sweet? Do you prefer soft or rough? (pause briefly)

It is. Begin eating your food. Be aware of the changes it makes. Utilize your entire mouth to look at the changes. If you're ready then tell me your observations and the food you had!

4. Alter roles when you want and let your child serve a meal onto your tongue while you attempt to figure out what the food is.

MASTER MINDFULNESS TIP: Change the exercise to suit the needs of your child. Certain children may want to focus their attention or discuss the things they're noticing and say it out loud. Your child is the authority on your child's behavior, therefore be sure to follow them.

Name That Sound

5-10 mins

The aim of this game is to allow your child to get connected to their sense of hearing. Making a habit of noticing sounds can be the best way to be connected to the present. As we become more immersed present in this moment as we practice, the more conscious you become.

BENEFITS: Focus & Attention, Executive Functioning Skills

Materials: Home appliances Nature sounds

1. Take a few items from your home to create various sounds for example, a pan or pasta box. There are also a variety of sound effects from nature on YouTube or even your mobile.

2. Your child should close their eyes.

3. Play or make different sound effects. After each sound, challenge your child to determine which sound it was.

4. Play around with this exercise while closing your eyes, while your child makes diverse sounds to please you.

5. Repeat the same thing as you want, using the same things or sounds that the child and you imagine.

Master Mindfulness Tips: Play the game outside during a sunny day! You can sit in a park within your own yard, and attempt to listen for different soundings around your. Try to guess the origin of each sound.

Iceberg Rescue

15-20 minutes

The activity increases the sense of touch in your child by bringing a powerful sensation to the touch --by touching something cold! It also allows your child to engage to their sensory senses in the present. Be aware that this task requires some preparation prior to the activity.

BENEFITS: Focus & Attention, Emotional Expression & Regulation, Mind-Body Connection

Materials AREA: Ice cube tray tiny plastic toys; plastic bin, or bowl in any shape; spray bottle, pitcher or measuring cup

1. In preparation for the activity to prepare for this activity, gather a selection of plastic toys that are compact enough to fit into an the ice cube tray (for instance, Legos, counting bears and bugs, mini-cars).

2. The ice cube tray should be filled with water, then place an item in each of the sections. Place the tray into the freezer till the toy has totally frozen.

3. Take the ice cubes out of the tray and put them into the bin. While you're doing this you do this, ask your child questions regarding the texture, temperature and feel of the cubes asking questions like: Do you feel your fingers are warm or cold whenever you hold the cubes?

4. Provide your child with a vessel that you are comfortable with pouring water from like a tiny water bottle or pitcher and measuring cups.

5. Encourage your child to try their hand on rescuing toys stuck within the frozen cubes of ice.

Continue to play Keep playing: This is an excellent way to learn the skill that lets your kid be the leader. You can let them take the charge of saving their toys, while you are able to announce each step you take! Keep them entertained and present by observing them at eye and level.

The Push It 3-5 minute time limit

If a child feels overwhelmed or angry, they are less likely to live in the present moment. Engaging in activities that trigger the nervous system, especially via proprioceptive inputs, help to ground the body. Proprioceptive input is the method by which our bodies move in space and our ability to perceive how we are in motion. Kids may struggle with this because of a range of causes. Push It is a game that Push It could cause an impression of substantial work on the body. It can also turn onto the proprioceptive systems and bringing the body into the present.

BENEFITS: Grounding & Coping Skills, Present-Moment Awareness, Calm & Relaxation

1. Ask your child whether they would like to make use of all their strength in order to push you down or push on the walls of your home.

2. If they decide to go with the house choose one wall to be attempting to move. Tell them to put their feet solidly on the floor and then use all their strength to and strength, knock the wall down!

3. If they prefer for you to sit, make sure that you facing each other. Based on your size, age, and ability of your child it is possible to choose to either remain in a sitting position or standing. Lock your hands together with your child's. Ask your child to force towards your hands with every ounce of strength.

4. When they are done pushing after which, encourage them to breathe deeply for two breaths, breathing slowly and then exhaling.

Master Mindfulness Tip: Have your child keep their breath in sync with their movements. Make them take a deep breath before starting pushing, and exhale all the time they push.

Mindfulness Jar

5-10 mins

Instructing children to read their body signals so that they can satisfy their desires can be a great approach to assist them in building awareness of their body sensations. The mindfulness jar is one of the most effective ways to achieve this.

BENEFITS: Mind-Body Connection, Impulse Control

MATERIALS: Jars or containers that is of any sort, food beverages, fidget toys trinkets and trinkets. Ice sandwiches, pop sticks

1. Choose items you are confident about letting your child anytime time. Select only items you feel confident that you will be able

to answer "yes" to. They should be able to fulfill the various needs your child could require, such as drinks, snacks, and water cups, in addition to items that cater for children's sensory needs (for instance, popcorns Paper, Play-Doh, or even a tiny bag of Legos).

2. Then fill the jar up with things and describe what it does:

Learning to become mindful master. The best way to achieve this is by paying attention to what you require right now. There are times when you need an alcoholic beverage or sweet treat. A different time it could be a specific toy or something you can take out! It is possible to use the items inside the jar whenever you'll need they. If you're in need of to use them they will be a yes!

Master Mindfulness Tips Give the jar nighttime time! This could happen after the brushing your teeth. Perhaps you're thinking, the yes jar always has a time for bed, the same as you! After the yes jar is at rest, we will not access things through it.

Layers of Sound

5-10 mins

It is a difficult yet effective method for your child to be connected with the sounds that surround the them, and then bring them to the present. Your child will be guided to hear sounds that originate from different distances. Start by hearing distant sounds and shifting to sound that is close.

BENEFITS: Present-Moment Awareness, Focus & Attention, Calm & Relaxation

1. Make sure your child is seated in the floor or in a chair or lay on a sofa.

2. Have your child close their eyes if they're comfortable in doing so.

3. Take them through the following steps and read them with a quiet, calm voice:

a. Breathe deeply through your nose, then take it out with your mouth. Try to take your listening all out to the outside of our home. Try to discern the sound outside. (pause briefly)

b. Bring your attention towards the interior of the house. You should be able to detect an echo in the interior. (pause briefly)

C. Check to see if you are able to reduce your listening the smallest of spaces or even inside of the. Try to discern the sound of your breath, or even the beat of your heart. (pause briefly)

D. Allow your listening to extend across the entire space. Breathe deeply and close your eyes.

4. Discuss with your child the various sounds that they have were hearing and how they felt. Discuss what was effortless or difficult during this activity.

Master Mindfulness Tip Based on your child's age as well as their capacity to concentrate it might be helpful to ask your child to write down the things they observe at the end of each step.

Feelings Song

3 to 5 minutes

An easy way to show your child to handle overwhelmed emotions is to demonstrate the various techniques you use when getting overwhelmed. This exercise teaches the participant a fun and efficient method to manage your emotions that are overwhelming you and helps your child develop the ability to manage their emotions.

BENEFITS: Grounding & Coping Skills, Emotional Expression & Regulation

1. If you're overwhelmed, listen to the following tune (to the beat of "London Bridge Is Coming Down"). Change the lyrics to express what you're experiencing:

I'm feeling extremely mad I am really, truly, crazy. I'm really angry this moment. It is possible to breathe or stop and take a break. make breaks. You can take a breath or even take a break today. (pause to breath)

2. While you are singing this song take the time to think about other steps that you can take to ease the stress like the ability to breathe, cry or taking a break away from the problem.

3. The song can also be modified song to assist your child recognize the emotions they feel in this moment. You can do this by naming a couple of feelings that you may feel:

Are you feeling angry or sad? Or mad? sad, sad or mad? Do you feel angry or sad at the moment? You are welcome to feel this in that manner. Feel it or feel the way. You can feel this in the moment.

MASTER Mental Health Tips Song this tune whenever you're struggling with staying cool. When you finish, speak up the way your body and attitude have changed since the performance.

Ring-a-Ding-Ding

3 to 5 minutes

This simple and quick game is an excellent opportunity to learn how to pay the attention of others. Utilizing simple objects at home, both the child and you will be focusing on the sound you can hear.

BENEFITS: Impulse Control, Focus & Attention

Materials: spoon and a pot, bell or chime

1. Pick an item you've got in your house which you could use to create a ringing or the sound of a ding. The spoon and a pot or a bell of any sort, or any other item available.

2. Then, tell your kid that the purpose of this game is to maintain their body still until the tone ceases.

3. Relax and take a deep breath with your partner.

4. When you and your child exhale make a splash or sound the bell. Instruct your child to

hold their position until the sound has completely gone.

5. Have a turn, and have your child playing the item the next. If you're using more than one objects, check which are more resonant.

Keep playing: You could modify the rules of this game with a motion or dance you and your child perform until the sound ceases. You could also play a game of guessing by letting one participant close their eyes while listening to the sounds, and then try to figure out which object caused the sound.

Music Hide-and-Seek

5-10 mins

This is an enjoyable twist on the traditional children's game of hunt-and-seek. The game helps children focus on the sounds around them in the present. If we provide opportunities for our children to be aware of only one sensory system at one time it helps the child develop awareness.

BENEFITS: Focus & Attention, Impulse Control, Present-Moment Awareness

Materials These include: Wireless Bluetooth speaker, mobile phone or music box

1. Select a device that plays music that you can feel at ease with the child's hands and hiding in your house.

2. You must decide which of you is going to be the hider, and who will be the hunter.

3. The device should be set to begin with music of all kinds in a level you are at ease.

4. The searcher shuts his eyes. The person who hides the device and conceals it away in their house.

5. In the classic game of hide-and-seek the player remains in his place and closes his eyes until the hiding party returns or, alternatively, until the player reaches the number ten.

6. The seeker attempts to track the sound, and find the device hidden.

7. After the seeker has located the device, change roles to play the game again.

Master Mindfulness Tips Make it more challenging by decreasing the volume of sound that is coming out of the device, or playing sound that is difficult to identify, like the sound of birds chirping, white noise or recordings of household sounds.

Artist Eyes

5-10 mins

This activity's goal is to allow your child to develop the habit of observing the world with an untrained mind. Achieving one of the pillars of mindfulness at one time can be a fantastic approach to improve your mindfulness. The game requires concentration as well as creativity. This is an excellent combination to learn the art of the beginning minds.

BENEFITS: Present-Moment Awareness, Focus & Attention, Creativity & Flexible Thinking

Material for coloring

1. Select a room within your house or safe outdoors space for the event.

2. Let your child explore the area and take note of all the things in the room. Ask them to make a visual within their minds of every object.

3. Get out of the area and head to another location. Make sure you have coloring materials on hand.

4. Try to get your child drawing as many of the details of the room that they just walked into as they possibly can. The goal is to draw a precise image of the area without having to look back.

5. When the drawing is completed After the drawing is completed, return to the drawing and ask your child to compare it with the space in order to determine how similar they are.

Master Mindfulness Tips: Let your child visualize the activity within their minds. Encourage them to create an image of the area, then put their eyes closed, then try to visualize and write down every aspect. Visualization is a sophisticated and demanding skill for adults and kids Don't fret that your child will need to master this skill.

Animal Dance

5-10 mins

The game takes a twist on the old-fashioned game called Simon Says. When we're challenged to combine attentive listening and moving, we're developing awareness and impulse control abilities. This game can be a delightful and fun way to set the challenge your child needs.

BENEFITS: Self-Compassion & Confidence, Focus & Attention

1. Discuss the rules for the game. The one of you is the animal, while one of you is the person who calls. It is the goal of the caller to

for animals to perform in the inappropriate time.

2. If you're the one calling Begin the game with saying "All animals dance! The animal, your child is then expected to dance in reaction.

3. When your child is dancing identify a variety of animals, items such as food, or places like, for instance that all chairs dance all waterfalls dance, every cookies dance, or even all dogs dancing.

4. Animals can dance in the event that the person calling it calls"the name" of any kind of animal.

5. If a pet dances at an inappropriate time If they dance in the wrong time, they're not allowed to dance! Play the game once more.

Chapter 6: Imaginative Stories & Metaphors

Children naturally utilize their imagination to process and control their experience and their world around them. The exercises in this chapter assist children to develop this ability while integrating the concept of mindfulness. The use of metaphors in some activities is an effective and simple method for children to gain the awareness of what mindfulness means. Some activities are focused on enhancing the skill of mindfulness through visualization using guided imagery, which can be walked through in a way that is developmentalally appropriate. The chapter concludes with games that let your child consolidate what they've discovered about mindfulness through drama and engaging games. These activities enhance the bond that you have with your child, and as a result, improve confidence in their own abilities and regulate their emotions.

Puppy Mind

5-10 mins

Mindfulness is a challenging concept for children to grasp. Utilizing a metaphor as well as a playful activities is an excellent method to show them how to be in the current time. One of the main elements of mindfulness is becoming aware that our thoughts may be somewhat chaotic (like the puppy who is running all over) and learning to gently slow the mind down.

BENEFITS: Present-Moment Awareness, Impulse Control, Executive Functioning Skills

1. Discuss the idea about "puppy mind" by using the following analogy:

Our minds can be as a puppy. They're able to run really quick and move constantly moving around! Mindfulness can help our puppies discover how to pay attention only one object at an time.

2. Then, choose which puppy, and then who will be the mindful master.

3. The puppy's owner starts by becoming energetic in their barking, running and chasing and doing the most convincing puppy impression.

4. Within a couple of minutes The mindfulness teacher will then say"Freeze!.

5. The puppy might freeze. breathe deeply and then name something they've seen.

Master Mindfulness Tips: For additional challenge, try to see how your child can observe what's going on inside their head whenever they switch from being silly to quiet. This can help them begin to apply their mindfulness abilities in real everyday life.

Weather Report

5-10 mins

The activity makes use of weather in order to allow children to connect to their emotions and share them. The process of learning to comprehend and articulate our emotions can be an arduous task. A simple analogy such as the weather can be a wonderful method to assist your child understand the emotions they feel in the present moment.

BENEFITS: Emotional Expression & Regulation, Mind-Body Connection

Material: Color and paper materials

1. Define feelings with the help of this weather-related metaphors:

Everyone experiences different emotions. Some days we feel heavy and stormy, while times we are bright and clear. There are times when we feel a bit sun-kissed, while sometimes we experience rain in the mornings while the sun shines later in the day. Our feelings are all acceptable and appropriate. The way we feel does not indicate whether or not we're positive or negative. They provide information to help us know what we need.

2. Let your child play with the papers and coloring supplies to draw a picture which reflects the kind of weather that they're

experiencing in the present. Anything goes, there's no right or wrong approach to doing this.

3. When your child is finished with the weather report Follow up with them throughout the day and check if there is anything new.

Continue to play: Do this exercise as soon as your child comes back from school, to think about and share their feelings about the day. Sometimes, talking about what you feel is difficult but it is more comfortable to express our emotions by drawing them out in a way.

Body Investigator

5-10 mins

The ability to feel the bodily sensations that we experience in our body is an ongoing challenge to anyone of any stage of life. It's a vital ability, as these feelings are a way to determine our physical needs as well as emotional. Mindfulness allows us to notice these feelings in the present and then figure out ways to make use of the information they provide. This exercise provides a simple and fun metaphor for explaining the concept to kids.

BENEFITS: Mind-Body Connection, Emotional Expression & Regulation

Material: Color and paper materials

1. The first step is to explain the concept:

Imagine a tiny body-observer that is inside the body. The job of this investigator is to aid us in finding the way our body feels. There are sensations in our body that reveal what we feel like, such as hot, cold or hungry. Also, we experience sensations in times of emotion. For instance, if we are anxious and sweaty, it is normal to feel. You can consult your body therapist to explain what our body's sensations are to help us determine what we're in need of.

2. Use your child's artwork materials and imagination to draw the image they believe

their body investigator is like. Anything is possible!

3. After they've drawn a sketch of their body examiner and their body investigator, they can continue to use the metaphor

The body's inspector has several modes to toggle on or off. Occasionally, the investigator is operating in "silent mode" and we do not be aware of what the sensations we feel or what we want. Sometimes, we may have our investigators switch on "notice mode" to help us to notice what's taking place in this moment, and also what we are in need of!

4. Let your child spend time working on asking the body's investigator to switch into "notice mode" with a simple command:"Activate notice mode!

5. After your child has enrolled in "notice mode" ask them to scan their body to identify a sensation that is felt somewhere. This could be as simple such as the feeling of their feet

on the seat, or more complex, such as the way your stomach feels.

6. Help your child utilize specific terms to describe the feelings, like sharp, hot, tight and stiff. They can be dull freezing, tingly or frozen.

MASTER MINDFULNESS TIPS When you speak more about this concept more often, the simpler it is for the child you love to pay attention to their body's sensations. Encourage them to turn on "notice mode" during different periods of the day in order to discover what their body is feeling.

Thought Boats

15-20 minutes

An enjoyable way to enhance the understanding of a child about mindfulness is to create something tangible and concrete. The concepts of mindfulness are usually abstract and therefore difficult for children to grasp. This exercise can help your child learn the practice of mindfulness, which is observing thoughts, without being overwhelmed with the thoughts.

BENEFITS: Self-Compassion & Confidence, Emotional Expression & Regulation

Materials: Small pieces of paper, such as pencils, sticky notes and other objects that contain small pieces of paper and even be floating (like smaller bowls, small cups or plastic caps for bottles, or tiny bath toys floating on the water) Large plastic containers

1. Encourage your child to write down the thoughts that they've had previously or currently experiencing. Note these thoughts on smaller scraps of paper. Make each thought piece into a tiny ball.

2. Ask your child to choose smaller objects which can be able to flot in their mind boats. Then, place the crumpled balls of paper inside the vessels.

3. In the container, fill it with water. Put the thought boats into the water.

4. The metaphor can be explained using this example:

Our minds are as this water. It is filled with a myriad of thoughts as these thoughts boats moving around. If we're mindful and aware, we attempt to look at the entirety of our thoughts, and not be swept away by the thoughts. It is easy to see that they exist, however we do not have to take action or even try to get rid from them.

5. Have a turn taking deep breaths, and then blowing the thoughts boats in the ocean.

Master Mindfulness Tips: When your child blows floating thought boats across the lake Have them try to spot the boats without having to guess or keep track of the thoughts each has carried.

I Am a Tree

3 to 5 minutes

A fantastic way to develop mindfulness for children is teaching them to imagine in their minds. An easy and developmentally appropriate method to achieve this is to read the children a captivating narrative. Get together and reading to them with your most gentle voice, and encourage them to develop this skill.

BENEFITS: Creativity & Flexible Thinking, Stress & Anxiety Management, Calm & Relaxation

1. Find a comfy spot for cuddling.

2. Your child should be asked to switch to their inner world and think about the possibility of closing their eyes.

3. Listen to the instructions below out loud:

a. Take a deep breath in.

b. Then imagine that you're the tree. Assume you're developing roots that reach down to the earth and branches that reach in the air. Imagine how your tree will look like. What is the color of your bark? Are they smooth or soft? What kind of leaves are you using? Which color do they come in?

C. Imagine what it would be like being so large and at such a height! What are you noticing that high up in the air?

D. Do a deep breath, then open your eyes.

4. Let your child tell you the things they observed and how it was like as in the tree. The questions to ask include:

a. How did your tree appear like?

b. Did your tree bear buds, leaves, or blooms?

C. What was it like to think of that you were the tree?

Continue to play: Take your coloring supplies and paper and let your child create a sketch of what they observed. It will allow them to further develop their visual skills.

Movie Magic 5-10 minutes

The purpose of this exercise is to teach your child how to make use of visualization for solving a problem. It has been proven that when we envision our own accomplishments in completing a assignment or solving a difficult problem that we're more likely to succeed when it comes to solving problems later on.

BENEFITS: Creativity & Flexible Thinking, Executive Functioning Skills

Materials: Coloring and paper materials

1. As you talk to your child, pinpoint the problem or issue they're experiencing. It could be as simple for example, such as finishing math homework, or it could be something significant, like learning to swim.

2. Then, ask your child to create a sketch of their own facing this task. The picture can be as imaginative or as dreamy as they'd like! Perhaps a fairy appears and assists them with their math assignments in the classroom, or they develop fish fins and gills in order to assist them in swimming. Anything is possible!

3. When they are finished sketching the image, let them visualize the scene as the movie that is being played in their heads.

4. Inspire your child to make fresh movies and artwork and come up with a new creative solution every time.

Master Mindfulness Tips: Try employing this method to your life, and take note of how it feels when you imagine yourself accomplishing something challenging by different means.

The Feelings Wave

3 to 5 minutes

The activity helps kids understand the way to feel emotions with the help of the simple concept of. Learning to be able to sense the emotions of others is a crucial and a powerful talent. All of us have emotions, and they are accepted and acceptable. It is easier for us to be capable of accepting and coping with our emotions as well as the problems of life if we are able to be aware of our emotions and withstand the waves of emotions.

BENEFITS: Emotional Expression & Regulation

1. The metaphor for the waves of feelings:

We all have emotions All of our emotions are accepted and acceptable. There are times when we feel angry, sad anxious, scared, joyful, exuberant and so on! The feeling doesn't last indefinitely. Feelings change and disappear. What's more? It is possible to be aware of our emotions as they occur and experience it as a surfer rides the waves. If we can do this, we can actually modify how we are feeling more quickly! The first step is to notice the feelings as they begin to increase. After that, we allow the sensation to persist. We then watch slowly shrink and then fade off.

2. Then, teach your child how to navigate the wave.

a. Feel the sensation: Identify your body's sensation within your body. Then, identify the place and what you feel. As an example, you could describe an uneasy feeling inside my chest.

b. Keep the sensation by breathing through and out, slowly, 3 times. Every time you breath in, think that your breath will travel into that area of your body. Try not to change the sensation. Simply let it stay there.

C. Be aware of the feeling Feel how your body experiences and feelings change within a couple of breaths.

3. Let your child experience through the waves of emotions repeatedly as often as they'd like until they feel like the emotion is something that they are able to handle!

MASTER MINDFULNESS TIPS: This can be an excellent tool to employ in times of feeling overwhelmed by the child's. The feeling wave may aid you in getting rid of anxiety and help you find a peaceful and grounded space.

My Favorite Color

3 to 5 minutes

This exercise helps develop the child's ability to focus with simple guided visualization. Find a comfy seat while breathing and keeping your mind on a single thing is an excellent opportunity to learn mindfulness.

BENEFITS: Creativity & Flexible Thinking, Stress & Anxiety Management, Calm & Relaxation

1. Find a cozy spot to snuggle.

2. Have your child turn to their inner world and think about the possibility of closing their eyes.

3. Listen to the directions in the following manner:

a. Inhale deeply through your nostrils. Then exhale it through your mouth. Make the sound of an AHH.

b. Visualize that the atmosphere surrounding you is visible and is your preferred color. Imagine that the air is full of things that will make you feel content and calm. You feel strong, confident and safe. Each time you take a breath your lungs, you're brimming with this color-filled air, and any other good things you wish for.

C. Take 5 or 6 deep breaths, and fill the air with as many color as we can.

4. Let your child tell you what colour they imagine. You can ask questions like:

a. What are the best things you could have in mind?

b. Which color did your most favorite affect you?

Master Mindfulness Tips This is an excellent exercise to perform prior to bedtime, helping your child achieve calm and peace before sleeping.

Imagine a World

15-20 minutes

We can find ourselves overwhelmed by the events that happens in our lives. Kids can be more assured of conquering a problem if they are involved in activities which help them feel confident. It is a fun method for kids to experience the strength and size of their bodies.

BENEFITS: Self-Compassion & Confidence, Creativity & Flexible Thinking

MATERIALS: Paper, coloring materials, blocks, Magna-Tiles, people figurines, Legos

1. Discuss how you plan to make an imaginary universe with each other. It is a world where anything is possible to be possible. Magical powers of any kind, particular powers, superheroes or mythical creatures are present!

2. Utilize any kind of materials available or the one your child is most comfortable with to build this world. Make use of the blocks and Legos to create a world which you are able to

engage with, or you can use markers and paper to draw diverse regions of the world.

3. When the world is constructed, you can work with your child to create a narrative about the world. Your child can be asked concerns such as:

a. Who are the people who live in this world?

b. What kinds of issues are present?

C. If something is wrong then who will solve the issue?

4. Listen to what your child makes up things such as This World is filled with many guardians! Assist them with their level, and observe their example.

Master Mindfulness Tips: Once you have completed the task then close your eyes. ask your child to close their eyes and think about the world around you. Try to describe diverse aspects of the world.

Animal Sidekick

3 to 5 minutes

The purpose of this exercise is to aid your child build an internal belief in themselves. Engaging in imagination and creativity by using visualization can be a fantastic method to boost the self-confidence of a child.

BENEFITS: Creativity & Flexible Thinking, Self-Compassion & Confidence

1. Find a cozy spot to snuggle.

2. Your child should be asked to switch into their own world of imagination, and then think about the possibility of closing their eyes.

3. The following instruction is read out loud:

a. Breathe deeply in the air, and then exhale it.

b. Most superheroes have an accompanying character. Imagine you own an animal friend. What kind of animal does it belong to? Does it look big or small? Do you see fur or scales?

Are you sure it's real or just an imagined one? How can you get in touch with your pet?

C. Imagine you and your companion are a couple, ready to conquer the world! How do you feel having the confidence that you will be able to accomplish the same thing?

D. Do a deep breathe in and let go. Relax your eyes until you're prepared.

4. Ask your child to share with you the things they imagine and describe how it felt to have the animal as a sidekick.

Keep playing: Let your child draw a sketch of their animal friend. Encourage them to think of the scenario in which their pet could be able to help to assist them in.

Stuffy Talks

Three to five minutes

It can often be difficult for children to communicate the emotions they're experiencing or how an experience went to them. Playing with or using fun objects is an excellent method to aid children in learning how to communicate. The activity makes use of toys to let kids to discuss their feelings without being required to talk about the feelings they feel.

BENEFITS: Emotional Expression & Regulation, Creativity & Flexible Thinking, Parent/Caregiver-Child Connection

Materials Animals that are stuffed

1. Find a couple of toys.

2. Your child and you will communicate with toys. Imagine that the animals talk, or you are able to read their minds and communicate with the animals.

3. The stuffed animals should ask one another questions. They can talk any topic. In the case of example, if your child feels worried or worried about an imminent date, make one of the pet ask the other animal how they feel about the coming occasion. It could be something like Bunny I've heard that you're

about to move to a different school. What do you think of it?

4. Continue to talk the duration of time your child's interest is high or until it makes you feel good.

Continue to play When you've talked about the upcoming event that is of concern Bring the animal that appeared to "speak" to your child at the time of the occasion. Check in with the pet as you go.

Ceiling Watch

3 to 5 minutes

Laying back on the floor while our feet are pressed against the wall is an ideal way to ease the body and soothe your nervous system. This body place into a chance to be creative and playful and can build the joyous, conscious connection between your child and you.

BENEFITS: Calm & Relaxation, Parent/Caregiver-Child Connection, Creativity & Flexible Thinking

1. Find a suitable and easy place for you as well as your child to lay on your backs in front of the wall. Begin walking slowly towards the wall until your legs can be stretched comfortably while keeping your feet's soles in front of the ceiling. If you find this posture uncomfortable the child or you could choose to lie down on the floor, feet resting on a sofa or chair.

2. Instruct your child to utilize your imagination to pretend the ceiling acts as a doorway into another dimension.

3. As you work together, visualize all the various things that you could observe. Your child can ask inquiries about the world like:

a. What can you imagine? (trees and water or even a mountain from candy?)

b. What kind of stuff is in the world? (animals, people, fairies, superheroes?)

C. What's the conditions like?

4. Keep in the position for about 3 to 5 minutes while you discuss the world around you.

MASTER Mindfulness Tips: Don't be a slave to taking deep breaths! Take three to five deep breaths in a row between the beginning and the close of the exercise.

Magic Carpet Ride

3 to 5 minutes

The purpose of this exercise is to assist your child achieve peace through an active imagination. Guide them through this enjoyable and simple guided visualisation for enhancing their mindfulness.

BENEFITS: Creativity & Flexible Thinking, Stress & Anxiety Management, Calm & Relaxation

1. Find a cozy spot for cuddling.

2. Your child should be asked to switch to their inner world and think about shutting their eyes.

3. The following instruction is read out loud:

A. Relax your breathing into and out.

b. Imagine you are on an amazing carpet of color. It's beautiful and filled with love, color and security. Imagine yourself walking across the carpet. It's soft and comfortable and the perfect dimension for you!

C. Your carpet is beginning to take off and takes you up in the sky. It flies effortlessly through soft fluffy clouds. Feeling light, free and peaceful. Then you realize the fact that all your anxieties, fears and worries are hidden in the clouds. Continue to rise in the skies!

D. Once you're set to take off in the ground, breathe deeply into your lungs and then glide across the magic carpet down to the floor.

4. Ask your child to share with you the things they witnessed and what they feel following their magical carpet trip.

Master Mindfulness Tips The following is a fantastic exercise to perform prior to bedtime or prior to the time a child begins the homework.

Sticky Thoughts

Three to five minutes

This activity's goal is to assist your child think about shifting their mood. While all emotions are neutral, so it's recommended not to categorize them as positive or negative but we could benefit in modifying the mood of certain people. In particular, anxiety might be "sticky," like we are unable to get them out of our minds. It's a great method to assist your child recognize a problem and then work to free themselves from the issue.

BENEFITS: Emotional Expression & Regulation, Calm & Relaxation

MATERIALS: Bubble liquid (optional)

1. We all worry, and often worry can be like they're stuck inside our minds and it is impossible to get out of them.

2. The breath we breathe is so potent, it helps us to send anxiety away.

3. You as well as your child select something that you're worried about.

4. It's time to let go of those ideas. Your child should be guided through these steps (have the bubble solution prepared and ready, if you are using):

a. Let your voice be heard over the fear which is causing you anxiety. (For instance, I'm anxious about visiting the doctor.)

b. Take a deep breath in. The breath you take will help to find the worry that is stuck.

Chapter 7: Play Therapy For Parents

Play therapy is a type that is specifically designed for children, which uses play as a method of communicating and healing. It's a non-directive method which allows children to be themselves through games, while providing children with a safe and supportive setting in which they are able to explore and work through the emotions, feelings as well as issues.

As as a parent, you may apply play therapy methods to help you understand and assist your child's needs for emotional support. Here are some suggestions for incorporating strategies for play therapy in the relationships you share with your child

Establish a secure and secure environment: It's crucial to provide an safe and hospitable environment in which your child is at ease expressing their feelings. Make sure you have a private and peaceful area in which you and your child are able to be together and play without interruptions.

Let Your Child Lead the Way Follow Your Child's Lead: Play therapy is a non-directive method, meaning that your child is the one who leads the activity. Be aware of what your child enjoys engaging in and follow them. It is possible to ask questions, ask for feedback or think about the things you observe.

Utilize Play as a Method for Communication: Play is a great means for children to talk with others, show their emotions, and explore their emotions. Let your child engage in play and let their imagination run free of charge. It is possible to ask questions that are open-ended like "Tell me about the drawing you made" or "What do your dolls are doing?"

Reflect on the feelings of your child If your child is expressing their emotions through playing, be aware and reflect on what you notice. Like, "I can see that you're angry due to the fact that you're throwing blocks." It helps the child to feel heard and respected.

Pay attention and be present Be Present and Attentive: Play therapy demands your attention and being attuned to the needs of your child. Beware of distractions such as phones and television, and instead focus on the game and interacting with your child.

To encourage creativity: Aid your child's imagination by giving them various materials as well as toys. Drawing, painting as well as sculpting, are all excellent ways for children to express their creativity.

Be patient Practice patience: Play therapy is a journey, and it can need time for your child's personality to come out and become at ease. Keep a steady and patient attitude when you try to help your child's emotional wellbeing.

Be aware that playing therapy isn't substitute for therapy provided by professionals It's a means to aid your child's psychological development and overall well-being. If you are concerned about the mental health of your child it is crucial to get the assistance of qualified mental health professionals.

Some examples that can help you understand the role of play therapy and the ways parents can apply the concepts to aid their children.

One example: A child that is suffering with anxiety

Perhaps your child is stressed and has trouble sleeping during the time of night. Play therapies to assist your child express and deal with their feelings. Make a space for relaxation within their room with soothing toys like fidget spinners or stress balls. Let your child play with these toys to engage with calming exercises like taking deep breaths or imagining.

Try playing games with your child, where they make an "worry monster" from clay or other substances. Have your child describe what the worry monster's appearance and feels like, as well as how it looks and how it functions. This will help them release their fears and develop the confidence to control the situation.

2. A child dealing with divorce

If your child goes through divorce or separation. Techniques for play therapy can help the child process their feelings and comprehend what's happening within an safe and happy environment. Create the "divorce box" for your child in which you can place photos, illustrations or objects that express their emotions or experiences of the divorce.

It is also possible to use game-based role playing to teach your child about the different viewpoints as well as develop empathy. You can, for instance, have a fun game in which you and your child takes turns as every family member, and then talk about what they may be experiencing or the things they may have been experiencing.

3. A child that is having difficulty with social abilities.

Perhaps your child has trouble with social abilities and finds it difficult to meet new people. The techniques of play therapy could help your child develop the social abilities, empathy, as well as communication abilities.

It is possible to arrange play dates with your children, and also encourage your child to participate in activities that require cooperation including making blocks, or playing games with board.

It is also possible to play games that can help your child develop compassion and an understanding of various viewpoints. As an example, you could engage in a game where the child is blindfolded, then you'll give them directions for how to finish an assignment. It can aid your child to comprehend what it's like to trust others, as well as how to communicate effectively.

In the end, play therapy is a potent method for parents to aid the children's psychological development as well as their overall wellbeing. In making sure that they create the conditions for a safe and friendly environment by following your child's direction by playing as a way to communicate, and expressing the emotions of their children, parents can aid their children to process their feelings, develop social skills, as well as gain the control they have in their lives.

The Importance of Play in Child Development.

The importance of play is a vital aspect of the child's development since it offers the opportunity for a fun and easy method for children to develop and develop. Through play, children can develop intellectual, social emotional, physical, and mental abilities that are essential for their general well-being and achievement throughout their lives. Here are the most important advantages of playing for children's development:

Learning to be Social: The game gives the opportunity for children to engage with others and develop social skills like collaboration, communication, negotiation and problem-solving. Through playing, kids learn how to interact with others as they share and play with each other, have a turn and communicate their thoughts as well as ideas.social development is a critical aspect of playing that assists youngsters learn how to connect with other children and develop connections. Through play, children acquire essential social skills like cooperation, communication as well as negotiation and problem-solving.

Collaboration: Play is a great way for children to cooperate to achieve a common goal. When, for instance, children construct a tower using blocks, they must collaborate and work together in ensuring that the building stays steady. Children learn to collaborate and develop an understanding of cooperation.

Communication: Play offers opportunities for kids to develop the skills of communication, like listening, speaking as well as expressing ideas and emotions. As an example, when kids are playing pretend, they have to be able to communicate in order to determine the roles they'll play and the rules for the game.

Negotiation: Play offers opportunities for kids to understand to bargain and negotiate in a group. As an example, if children are playing a game they could need to compromise rules, or play with others in order to make sure that all players have the chance to participate. Children develop the necessary skills to solve conflict and deal with real-world circumstances.

Problem-solving: Games provide opportunities for kids to develop the ability to think through problems like analyzing situations as well as generating solutions and test them. When children are playing with puzzles, they have to look over the puzzle pieces, and determine the best way in order to solve the puzzle.

In the end Social development by playing helps kids learn to communicate with each other, develop empathy and understanding and develop positive relationships. Additionally, it provides an safe and a supportive space where children can practice and improve their social skills that will be crucial to their performance in working, school, and in life.

Learning and Development through Play: Playing is a great way to stimulate the brain, and it helps youngsters develop abilities in cognitive development including the ability to focus, memory, perception as well as imagination. Children also develop the ability to think in a creative manner to solve issues, as well as develop abstraction skills.Cognitive development is a crucial component of children's progress as well as development Play plays crucial roles in developing the cognitive abilities of children. As children playing, they utilize their imaginations and talents to discover their surroundings and comprehend the world around them. Children learn new concepts as well as problem-solving and the ability to think critically.

These are a few ways games can aid in the development of the cognitive development for youngsters:

Exploring the World through Play lets children explore and discover their surroundings. A child, for instance, playing with blocks of all kinds can discover dimensions, shapes as well as colors, and develop their spatial skills.

Inspiring Imagination: Play allows kids to utilize their imagination and to think in a creative way. For instance, pretend play can help children imagine imaginative situations and develop their storytelling abilities.

Developing problem-solving skills The game provides the opportunity for children to work through issues and take decisions. As an example, a child playing a game on the board needs to consider the best strategy to prevail in the game.

Developing attention and memory: The brain is stimulated by games and assists youngsters develop the ability to pay attention and develop memory. A child, for instance, playing a memory game needs to recall where each of the cards is set to be able to win.

In the development of mathematical concepts, play gives children the chance to develop the fundamental math concepts including counting, sorting and the measurement. A child using a puzzle helps develop their spatial thinking skills and is taught to identify dimensions and shapes.

As a conclusion, playing can be a powerful tool for encouraging the cognitive development among youngsters. Through playing, kids can develop the ability to solve problems as well as their attention, memory, creativity, as well as mathematical thinking. In providing their children with the opportunity to play, parents and caregivers can aid their children develop important cognitive capabilities and help them succeed later in life.

The development of emotions through play helps children explore and manage their emotions essential for the development of their psychological development. Through playing, kids learn how to deal with anxieties, stress and anger, as well as develop confidence in themselves, empathy as well as resilience.Play gives children the safe and comfortable environment in which they can communicate and control their emotions. This is vital to developing their psychological development. Here are a few ways in which play can help the emotional development:

Children can express themselves through play. to let their feelings out with ease and in a non-threatening manner. A child, for instance, might use puppets or dolls to express their emotions as well as sketch or draw to convey their feelings. Through expressive games, children gain an understanding of their feelings, and develop self-awareness.

Control: Play can help children develop the ability to manage their emotions as well as deal with anxiety and stress. As an example, a child might play with a stress ball or other toy that helps calm them for relaxation and to lessen their stress. Playing with toys, kids can also develop the ability to self-soothe and control their feelings and emotions in a safe manner.

Empathy: Play offers the opportunity for children to develop empathy as well as an understanding of the emotions of others. As an example, children might play around with different scenarios, and discover how they can imagine themselves in another's in their shoes. Through playing, kids can develop emotional and social intelligence and discover how to connect to others on a more personal scale.

Resilience: Through play, youngsters develop flexibility and resilience vital to the emotional health of children. In the example above kids may discover how to deal by losing a game or not achieving their goals when playing a game. Through playing, kids can be taught to overcome defeats and develop confidence in facing difficulties.

In the end, playing is an effective method for kids' emotional development. In creating an safe and a supportive space where children can express and manage their emotions, playing can assist children to develop awareness of themselves, empathy resilience and other vital emotions. Parents and caregivers can help support the children's psychological development by engaging them with their play by offering them with the right tools, as well as participating with them when it is appropriate.

Physical Development: Play offers kids with the chance to develop their gross motor abilities including jumping, running, and climbing. It also helps develop the fine motor skills like cutting, drawing and constructing. Playing sports also aids children to keep their weight in check, develop coordination, and enhance their general well-being as well as well-being.Physical games are an essential aspect of child development in that it provides youngsters with the opportunity to exercise through their body and develop the ability to coordinate and increase their general health and wellbeing. These are just a few benefits of physical activities to the children's development:

The Gross Motor Skills Play aids kids develop the gross motor abilities and involves massive muscle groups as well as whole body moves. The examples of Gross Motor abilities include jumping, running and climbing, throwing and catch. Through playing, kids develop endurance, coordination as well as balance and endurance. These are essential to their physical fitness.

Fine Motor Skills Physical activity aids children to develop the fine motor abilities which include small muscles and hand-eye coordination. Fine motor abilities include painting, drawing, cutting as well as building. Through play, kids develop the capacity to control objects, work with tools as well as perform precise movements, essential in their daily activities.

Self-regulation: Physical activity provides kids with the chance to manage their moods and behaviors that are crucial for their emotional and social development. Through playing, children develop the ability to regulate their emotions, adhere to the rules and interact with people in a respectful and positive and respectful manner.

The development of the brain through physical play can stimulate the brain and encourages the formation of neural connections. This plays a crucial role in children's brain development. Playing sports has been proven to lead with improved attention, memory as well as academic performance and also reduced anxiety and stress.

Overall health and well-being: Physical activity helps children keep an ideal weight, boost their cardiovascular health and lower their chances of developing the onset of chronic illnesses later in life. The physical activity also helps improve wellbeing and mental well-being through decreasing stress, enhancing mood and social connection.

Physical play is a crucial aspect of a child's development which contributes to a child's overall health as well as their overall wellbeing and performance throughout life. In encouraging children to engage with physical activities Parents and caregivers will be able to assist their children's physical social, cognitive and emotional development and provide their children with a stimulating as well as enjoyable experience in learning.

Play can provide the opportunity for children to develop the skills of language, like vocabulary, grammar, as well as pronunciation. It also helps children learn how to communicate effectively, listen actively, and understand social cues and nonverbal communication.Language development is a critical aspect of a child's overall development, and play provides an excellent opportunity for children to develop their language skills. While playing, children participate with a myriad of tasks that require interaction, for example, discussing ideas, bargaining as well as problem-solving. The play environment allows children to speak freely to ask questions and utilize words in an appropriate context.

Here are a few ways that play can support the language development:

Language: Play is a great way for children to acquire new vocabulary and increase their vocabulary. When children are playing with toys, such as animals, they are taught the names of species of animals as well as the sounds they produce.

The play environment lets children practice grammar in a natural, fun way. As an example, if kids play with dolls they talk to each other using pronouns, verbs as well as adjectives appropriately.

Pronunciation: Playing with children allows them to develop their pronunciation as well as develop clearly spoken speech. When children, for instance, sing songs, they will learn how to pronounce sounds and words accurately.

Skills for communication: The game offers kids with opportunities to work on their communications skills, including talking and listening. As an example, when kids interact with other children they are taught to share the load to listen attentively and communicate clearly.

Nonverbal and social cues The game of play allows children to understand social cues and nonverbal communication such as body expressions, facial expressions and the tone of voice. As an example, if children engage in games such as the game of charades, they are taught make use of nonverbal cues in order to convey messages and communicate.

As a conclusion, playing is a fun and easy method for kids to develop their communication skills. When they engage in activities that involve play kids can broaden their vocabulary, work on the pronunciation of their words, develop communication skills, as well as learn about how to communicate with others and social cues. Parents and caregivers can aid their child's language development through a range of activities and opportunities for play, as well as engaging in activities of play together with their children.

It is a crucial aspect of children's development which helps children develop intellectual, social physical, emotional and abilities that are essential for their well-being overall and for achievement in their lives. Through encouraging children to engage in play, parents as well as caregivers are able to support their children's growth and development and provide children with a fun and engaging learning experiences.

HISTORY OF PLAY THERAPY

The pioneers of psychotherapy for children were ones who initially explained the ways in which playing can be used as a tool as a treatment. The philosophical basis for playing was initially thought of by Melanie Klein (1961, 1987), Margaret Lowenfeld (1935, 1970) as well as Anna Freud (1928, 1964 and 1965). For example, Klein (1961, 1987) said that a child's spontaneity in play is a replacement for free association utilized in adult psychoanalysis.

With each form of psychotherapy for children There are a variety of the theories of play and their practices. It is the fundamental principle that play is a means of communicating a child's thoughts, feelings thoughts, feelings, and ideas in a way that is not conscious, unites all practices, but.

The unique theoretical basis of The Humanistic Psychology tradition and Attachment theory, the field of play therapy evolved out of aspects of psychotherapy for children.

Carl Rogers (1951, 1955) invented a different type of psychotherapy during the 1940s known as"client-centered therapy" (later referred to as individual-centered therapy). Contrary against the prescriptive and diagnostic perspectives of the moment this brand new method was created. It was important to establish a genuine reliable, tolerant, and trustworthy relationship between the therapist and the patient was highlighted. Thus, the approach of a person-centered one offered a new and distinctive conceptual perspective on personal development as well as psychological health as well as the appearance of psychological issues, as well as the transformation process in therapy.

Axline (1969 Axline (1969, 1971) invented non-directive play therapy as a unique therapeutic method to deal with children mostly because of the person-centered method. Axline came up with a specific, concise and concise method to play therapy based on the theories of person-centeredness. Her most well-known story is of working with a tiny boy called Dibs (Dibs in the Search for Self 1964). Axline was very detailed regarding her experience working with Dibs and the way he was eventually able to heal himself. No one is as informed about the person's life as they are the individual who is a part of them, she said. The capacity to be independent and accountable comes from within the person. A lot of play therapists rely on the eight principles of her therapeutic connection to guide them to their work.

Based on Clark Moustakas, the focus of his efforts is how to create the connection needed to enable counseling as a learning process. His stages begin with a child's thoughts generally negative and when they're expressed in a way, the force of those sentiments diminishes. In the end, positive emotions and friendships eventually begin to emerge.

In America the field of play therapy has been utilized and researched for over fifty years. A number of play therapists including Moustakas (1953 1966, 1983, 1993,), Schaefer (1976, 1986 1993) and Landreth (1991 2002) took the lead and have developed a variety of models which incorporate family therapy systemic the narrative therapy, treatment-focused therapy and cognitive behavior therapy. They've improved Axline's initial formulas.

The 1980s were when Play Therapy began to develop as a distinct and innovative style in Britain. It was the Children's Hour Trust first trained specialists in the basic practices that are part of the Axline's Play Therapy, which are employed in various scenarios. In parallel two therapists in the field of drama began in incorporating Play Therapy techniques into their sessions with children. In order to create an British Play Therapy movement, Sue Jennings and Ann Cattanach (1993 1994, 1998, 1993) utilized elements of the non-directive approach to play therapy. A Diploma and Certificate in Play Therapy was first offered in the year 1989 by the Institute of Dramatherapy.

Professionals enrolled in the Institute of Dramatherapy founded the British Association of Play Therapists (BAPT) in the year 1992. Since that time, BAPT has created the British Play Therapy movement and has been acknowledged as a recognized by UK as an accrediting supplier of education programs which include the Master-level training programs that are offered by the University of Roehampton (London) as well as the University of Glamorgan (Wales).

Presently, British Play Therapy is defined as follows:

It is a dynamic procedure that occurs between the child and a therapy therapist. The child explores at his pace and according to their own agenda current and past both conscious and subconscious issues which influence children's lives today. Therapy is a way to harness children's own capabilities to impact development and change. The primary channel is play as is speech, which happens to be the third one for child-centered play therapy.

Theory Underpinning Play Therapy

The patient is considered an honest participant in therapy through play. Three key theoretical concepts constitute the foundation for play therapy.

Actualization: Humans are born with an inherent capacity to develop powerful positive personality traits. The concept behind this is to reveal the potential of every person. This includes their talent for creativity in their pursuit of knowledge, curiosity as well as their desire to increase in independence and power.

The importance of positive regard All people should feel loved, appreciated, and loved by everyone around them especially by "significant other people." A desire for positivity is a second, learned need for confidence in oneself and self-esteem as children mature and develop.

Play as a Method of Communication. Play is the primary method of communication used by children. Children's beliefs, emotions thoughts, perceptions, and attitudes are conveyed by the play. Play is mostly an artistic medium.

Learning about play therapy

The study of play therapy is conducted from 1942, to study many different topics including clinical efficacy as well as parental involvement, and the study of particular strategies. The following research papers are summarized in this article to provide an overview of the entire corpus of research on play therapy:

The effectiveness of non-directive therapy for children who've experienced domestic violence was studied in Kot (1995). In 1995, the Joseph Pre-School and Primary Self-Concept Screening Test and the Child Behavior Checklist, and the Children's Play Sessions Behavior Rating Scale were utilized to compare the outcomes of a controlled group, and to evaluate their effectiveness. The children in the therapy group were observed to have less behavioral problems overall, and also with externalizing behaviours. The study included 20 children of this study, who ranged between 3 and 10 years old.

The effectiveness of art and play therapy for children with one parent suffering from problems with alcohol or drugs was investigated by Springer and co. in the year 1992. In 1992, there were 132 participants who participated in the study, which ranged in between 7 and 17 years old. It was found that hyperactive, depressive and disruptive behaviors in the treatment group significantly increased (identified through the Child Behavior Checklist).

Children who suffer from violent conduct disorder that attended 16 hours of non-directive play therapy, as well as counseling for parents showed significant behavioral improvements in accordance with Dogra as well as Veeraraghavan's (1994) study. Therapy groups showed significant improvement in their self-esteem, family and school life, as well as social emotional, and physical adjustments as assessed through the picture-frustration Test as well as the Child Behavior Rating Scale. The incidence of bullying, fights and aggression toward adults, anger, and compliance have all diminished in the study group. The study included 20 participants. this study. Their were ages varied from 8 up to 12.

A meta-analysis involving 94 research papers that examined the therapeutic value in play therapies was carried out by Ray and co. in 2001. The research conducted in 2001 looked at the impact on the effects of Play Therapy on 3263 people (mean age: 7.1 years) and they were conducted by specialists from mental health across America. All of the research utilized an experimentation-based approach. The effectiveness in the use of Play Therapy with various client groups was analyzed in research of 94. Twenty clients were studied, and problems such as conduct disorders anxiety/fear, speech and problems with language, depression, sexual assault, as well as post-traumatic stress disorder were among the topics which were studied. An effect size of significant (d=.80) was observed on the Ray et al. (2001) meta-analysis. The researchers concluded that play therapy can be a very effective treatment to a range of problems that affect children.

Apart from the studies that have been mentioned, a variety of studies were conducted in Britain. At present, most studies focus on qualitative evaluations of Play Therapy sessions to illuminate how exactly the process works in helping children overcome life's stresses by using playing the Play Therapy process. The amount of Masters and Ph.D. applicants that study the field of play therapy has significantly been increasing in recent times. Four of the universities with education programs that are recognized are also able to provide doctoral and master's research courses.

Chapter 8: Benefits Of Play Therapy For Children

It is a kind of therapy that utilizes the game of play in aiding children to express their feelings and work through issues and develop the ability to cope. The practice of play therapy is beneficial for kids dealing with various problems with their behavior and emotions such as depression, anxiety as well as trauma and developmental issues. Below are a few important benefits of playing therapy for children

The regulation of emotions: Play therapy allows children to explore their feelings in the context of a safe and a supportive setting. When they engage in activities that involve play kids can deal with challenging emotions and discover how manage emotion in a safe way.Play therapy is particularly efficient in helping children to learn how to control the emotions they experience in a positive manner. Children are often overwhelmed by feelings like sadness, anxiety, or sadness. They aren't equipped to let these feelings out effectively. Play therapy is the safe place for kids to express and explore their feelings through games that can aid them in discover how to manage their emotional states in a healthy manner.

In play therapy, kids are encouraged to engage in games as a way to express their feelings for example, by making artwork, building using blocks, or playing the drama of play. The therapist offers help and advice as needed and assists the child in learning to learn to handle their feelings within the most safe and healthy manner.

A child with anger issues might be taught to play with toys that permit the child to show their anger by hitting pillows or an object of violence. In this way children can be taught how to vent their anger in an safe and appropriate manner instead of hitting other people. The therapist can help the child develop methods to manage their anger. This could include slow breathing, or counting from ten to.

Through helping children understand how to manage their emotions with the play process, it will have lasting benefits. The children who understand how to control emotional issues in a positive manner are able to deal with stress, establish strong relationships with other people as well as excel academically and socially.

Learning to solve problems The play therapy program provides the opportunity for children to develop solving problems as well as develop different strategies for dealing problems. Through playing with different situations and exploring new ways of thinking youngsters will develop the ability to solve problems and boost their confidence.Play therapy can be especially beneficial for kids who have difficulty in solving problems. Through playing, kids can learn different ways to solve problems as well as develop different strategies for dealing with challenging circumstances. The play therapist can use various play equipment like dolls, puppets, games as well as art materials and the sand tray, which can help kids explore different situations and resolve issues.

There are a few ways in how play therapy could assist children develop the ability to solve problems:

Training: Play therapy gives kids with opportunities to test their solving problems within an safe and a supportive setting. Through play, kids can explore different strategies and make mistakes, without having to worry about failing or judging.

Creative play: The practice of playing therapy stimulates imagination and creativity, which helps children think out of the box, and find creative and novel ways to solve problems.

Metaphors: Play therapy typically employs metaphors, like the puppet show or Sand tray, in order to assist kids explore and deal with challenging emotions and circumstances. They can provide an safe and safe environment for children to investigate their feelings, and to find solutions for their issues.

Empowerment: The therapeutic use of play therapy can enable children to become the master of their own problems and come up with solutions on their own. When they engage in activities that involve play youngsters can develop confidence in their abilities to tackle problems and manage tricky scenarios.

Role-playing in play therapy: This can include role-play, in which children can play diverse roles and look at diverse views. It can assist the child to develop a better comprehension of the issue, as well as develop empathy towards others.

In the end, play therapy can be a successful instrument to aid kids develop the ability to solve problems. Through creating the children with a safe and comfortable environment that allows children to try out solving problems and to explore various strategies, play therapy could aid children in building confidence, imagination and courage even in the face of difficulties.

Communication skills: Play therapy is a great way to help children improve their communication skills in both non-verbal and verbal communication. Through playing, kids can develop the ability to communicate better, express their wants and needs and actively listen to others. Play therapy can be especially beneficial in helping children improve their communication abilities. Through play, children develop the ability to communicate more clearly and convey their feelings, thoughts, and wants in a healthy manner. There are a few ways that play therapy may assist in improving communication skills of children:

Communication through non-verbal means Play therapy enables children to communicate non-verbally via gestures, facial expressions and body expressions. If they are attentive to these signs therapy professionals can get a better understanding of the child's emotions and assist the child in learning to express and recognize their feelings.

Communication through play therapy: Play therapy will also aid children in improving their communication abilities. Through engaging in conversation with therapists during play the children are able to practice speaking in a clear manner and communicate their feelings and thoughts effectively.

The practice of active listening can aid children to develop their listening abilities. Through playing, kids will learn how to be attentive to other people, react appropriately to others, and demonstrate compassion and empathy.

Social communication. Play therapy can assist children develop their skills in social interactions like turn-taking, cooperating, and sharing. When they play with their peers, kids learn these abilities within an environment that is safe and a supportive setting.

Understanding emotions through play therapy helps children to understand and communicate their feelings more efficiently. Engaging in games that are centered around emotions, for example, role-playing or telling stories youngsters can be taught to identify their own emotions as well as other people's emotions as well as develop compassion and empathy.

In the end, play therapy is a powerful method to improve children's communications skills. Through play, children develop their verbal and nonverbal abilities to communicate, their active listening as well as social communication abilities as well as a better understanding of emotions. In order to improve their communication skills youngsters can develop better connections with their peers, share their emotions and desires more efficiently, and have an improvement in their mental wellbeing and overall health.

Social abilities: Play therapy may aid children to develop the social skills like the ability to cooperate, be compassionate, and respect for other people. Through playing in a group, kids can develop the ability to relate with peers with respect and in a positive way. Play therapy is a great way to help youngsters develop social abilities by giving them chances to connect with their therapist and fellow kids within an environment that is safe and supportive atmosphere. These are just a few methods that playing therapy helps develop social competence:

Cooperation: The activities of play therapy typically have children work in teams in order to accomplish a shared goal. Through working in a team they can develop the ability to be part of a team, play with each other working together, and even collaborate with colleagues.

Empathy: The practice of play therapy can assist children develop empathy through giving them the opportunity to comprehend and connect with the feelings and experiences of other people. Through play, children are able to examine diverse views as well as develop an appreciation for the needs and emotions of other people.

Respect for other people The therapeutic benefits of play therapy are that it helps youngsters develop respect for each other through providing opportunities to engage in positive and respectful interactions with their therapists and their peers. Through playing, kids can be taught to pay attention to others, behave respectfully and effectively communicate with other people.

Social problem-solving and play therapy can aid children to develop abilities to deal with social issues through providing chances to test different strategies to resolve conflicts and deal to social issues. Through play, children are able to experiment with various scenarios and develop how to handle social interactions effectively and in a positive manner.

Skills for friendship play therapy helps youngsters develop abilities to be friends by giving them the opportunity to make acquaintances as well as developing relations with other people. Through play, children be taught to engage in discussions, discuss ideas and hobbies and develop relationships to their friends.

Self-esteem: Play therapy has the potential to improve confidence in children's self-esteem. By experiencing success in play activities and receiving positive feedback from the therapist, children can develop a more positive self-image and increased self-esteem.Self-esteem is a crucial aspect of a child's emotional and psychological development, and play therapy can help to boost a child's self-esteem in several ways:

The benefits of play therapy offers children opportunities to be successful in a non-competitive and a safe atmosphere. If children are engaged in with a challenge but feasible, they will feel an inner satisfaction and feel confident of their capabilities.

Positive feedback: Therapists for play provide kids with positive evaluation and praise for their achievements and efforts when they the game. Positive reinforcements can assist boost confidence in a child's self-esteem and self-confidence.

Self-awareness and self-esteem: Play therapy will help kids become aware of their thoughts attitudes, and behaviours. Play therapy allows children to discover their feelings and gain about their own personalities. The increased awareness of self can assist to boost self-esteem through giving children an knowledge of their strengths and their weaknesses.

Expression of emotions: Play therapy offers children an safe and a supportive space for them to share their feelings. Through playing kids can communicate their emotions in a non-verbal manner, thereby helping in reducing anxiety and building confidence in themselves.

Learning to cope The play therapy program can assist youngsters develop strategies for coping the stress of difficult emotions and stressful feelings. If children develop efficient strategies for coping They can be more assured and competent in facing challenges.

This will help them build confidence in themselves.

In the end, play therapy is a great method to build confidence in children's self-esteem. Through providing the opportunity for achievement and positive feedback, as well as increased confidence in oneself, emotional expression as well as coping development playing therapy may aid children in feeling more secure and adept at tackling the challenges. Self-confidence will help kids excel throughout their lives. This includes relationships with others, academic achievement as well as personal development.

Therapy for trauma recovery play therapy is an effective method for helping children suffering from trauma. When they engage in activities that involve play kids can process their experience within an environment that is safe and secure environment. They can develop strategies for coping, and start the recovery process.Trauma has a profound effect on children's emotional and behavior, which can lead to conditions like depression, anxiety as well as difficulties sleeping or sleeping, as well as nightmares and anxiety-provoking thoughts. Play therapy may provide children with a safe and safe environment that allows children to process their emotional trauma as well as develop strategies for coping.

Below are some examples of ways that playing therapy may be beneficial in helping to heal trauma:

Safety: Play therapy creates the children with a safe and positive setting for children to talk about their feelings and deal with their experiences. Through providing an environment that children are safe and secure and safe, they will begin to trust their therapists and be more comfortable in talking about their feelings and thoughts.

Self-expression: Play therapy enables children to share their thoughts and experience through games. Kids can play with tools, toys or other play equipment to play out traumatic incidents and express emotions and process their emotions.

Skills for coping Therapy through play can assist kids develop strategies for coping with emotions and react to trauma. Through playing, kids can develop the ability to manage their moods, recognize their triggers and develop strategies for handling stressful circumstances.

Narrative therapy: The practice of play therapy employs narrative therapy to assist children in creating an encapsulated and coherent story of their experience. In exploring the meaning behind their experiences, and constructing an account that is meaningful for them, they can be able to begin to comprehend their experiences and begin to work towards the healing process.

Integration of the right and left brain: The practice of play therapy can aid children in integrating their right and left brain functions. This is crucial for the recovery from trauma.

Traumas can affect the function of the brain and lead to the disconnection of different brain areas. Children can participate in activities that stimulate both brain sides to promote healing and integration.

Play therapy could be a successful method to help children recover from trauma. Through providing children with a safe and comfortable environment to let their voice be heard, developing coping strategies development as well as narrative therapy and integration of left as well as right brain functions, playing therapy helps children to work through trauma and progress toward the healing process.

Here are some instances of ways that play therapy could be utilized to assist children overcome trauma.

Playing with toys can help express emotion The child who has been through trauma might have difficulty convey their feelings in a verbal manner. The play therapy program allows children to play with toys as well as other objects to express their feelings through non-verbal means. As an example, a child could use a toy in order to play out an emotional or painful experience, and to express feelings about the experience.

Playing role-play can help develop strategies for coping The practice of play therapy may be used to aid children in learning how to develop strategies for coping. As an example, a child might role-play an event in which they are confronted with a trigger linked to their anxiety or experience, then practice strategies for dealing with stress, like meditation or positive self-talk in order to control the emotions.

Sand tray therapy to aid in therapeutic narrative Therapy using sandtrays can be employed to aid children write a story about their own experiences. Children can use miniature objects in order to construct scenes that depict their experience as well as work with the therapy therapist to construct a cohesive narrative that is understood by the child.

Therapy for emotions It is a great way to assist children express their feelings through non-verbal means. As an example, a child can use art tools for drawing or painting to express their emotions about the trauma they have experienced.

Relaxation techniques based on play for control play therapy may be used to aid children in regulating their moods. As an example, a child could play with a sensory item like the stress ball or fidget spinner to aid in calming to their level and concentrate.

Here are a few instances of the numerous ways that the use of play therapy is a way to aid children in recovering from trauma. The exact methods used be based on the needs of the child and the therapy approach.

Play therapy has the potential to provide multiple benefits for youngsters, such as improvement in emotional regulation, problem solving abilities, communication skills social skills, self-esteem as well as trauma healing. In creating an safe and a safe space for children to play with play, therapy helps children conquer problems with their behavior and emotional issues, and achieve their potential to the fullest extent.

Supporting Your Child's Healing in Play Therapy.

As as a parent, you have many things you can do to help your child heal during playing therapy. Below are some suggestions on how to help your child:

Establish a secure and safe home environment: It's essential to provide an safe and secure home to your children. This could include setting clear boundaries, giving emotional support and an orderly routine. A supportive home environment can help your child feel secure and reduce the impact of any stressors they may be experiencing.Creating a safe and supportive home environment is a critical part of supporting your child's healing in play therapy. Kids who have been through trauma can experience fears, anxieties and fear, anxiety and. An safe and secure home helps children feel comfortable and minimize the effect on any anxiety or stressors they could have to endure. These are some of the strategies to help you make your home an environment that is safe and comfortable home:

Set clear Boundaries Set clear boundaries to set clear boundaries within the home in order to let the child to feel safe and safe. It could be as simple as setting boundaries around the screen time and establishing guidelines for behaviour and communication, as well as setting up a regular routine.

Offer emotional support children who have been through emotional trauma might experience fears, anxieties or sadness. Offering emotional support will aid your child in feeling more secure and decrease the effects of stressors that they are experiencing. You can do this by offering positive words of support as well as paying attention to the child's issues and expressing their emotions.

Establish a stable routine: Making a solid routine helps your child feel safer and minimize the effect of stressors that they might encounter. This could mean establishing an established bedtime routine, providing regular snacks and meals, and establishing a predictable timetable for appointments and activities.

Build positive relationships: Positive interactions between family, friends, as well as others who are supportive can make your child feel secure and minimize the effect on any anxiety or stressors they could experience. Encourage children to be able to enjoy time with people who are supportive is a great approach to aid in their recovery.

Create a calm and comfortable Ambience: It's important to provide the calmest and most comfortable atmosphere in your house to make your child feel safe and at ease. This could include creating an environment that is comfortable and peaceful where your child can relax as well as creating a calm ambience by lighting softly or soothing fragrances.

If you create your child's environment in a safe and supportive environment in your home You can make your child feel secure and lessen the effects on any anxiety or stressors they could experience. It can be a crucial element in aiding your child's recovery during play therapy as well as beyond.

Participate in Therapy Sessions Therapy sessions: Attending the therapy sessions of your child may be beneficial in many ways. You can be observant of your child's development as well as observe how they're dealing with their feelings. Additionally, it gives you an opportunity to gain knowledge and techniques from the therapist which you can apply to assist your child back at home.Attending sessions with your child can be crucial to help the healing process in therapy. There are a few specific methods that going to therapy could be beneficial:

Monitoring your child's development Through attending therapy sessions, you will be able to monitor your child's development and observe how they're managing their emotions. It is possible to observe what they do with therapy therapist, the objects or toys they are drawn toward, as well as how they games. It can provide you with the insight to how your child feels and the things they might require from your side in regards to support.

Techniques and methods for learning Sessions with therapists can provide you with the chance to gain strategies and methods from the therapist can help you support your child in their home. Therapists can provide your child with specific skills for dealing with stress or relaxation methods which you could practice at your home. Working with a counselor, you'll be taught how to aid the healing process of your child in a better way.

Establishing a more intimate relationship with your child by attending therapy sessions is the best way to establish relationships to your kid. Through participating in their process of healing it will show them that you care about the child, and you're there to support their needs. This will help increase confidence and increase the strength of your bonds.

Promoting the value of therapy. By participating in sessions of therapy alongside your child it is possible to show the value of seeking therapy whenever needed. It can decrease stigma surrounding mental illness and help instill confidence in your child's ability to seek out help when they require it.

It's important to remember that participating in therapy sessions with your child may not be required or necessary. Therapists might prefer working on a one-to-one basis with the child or suggest a few session with the family instead of frequent involvement. It is crucial to discuss the involvement you are taking therapy sessions with the Therapist and adhere to their suggestions.

Be a good listener and validate your child's emotions: It's crucial for you to pay attention to your child's feelings and validate the feelings they are experiencing. It is important to acknowledge the emotions of your child and telling them that you're there to assist your child. If you can validate the feelings of your child and letting them feel understood and heard and this can be essential to the process of healing process.Listening and confirming your child's emotions is essential to helping them heal through the play therapy. In the event that a child is experiencing trauma, they might struggle to communicate their feelings or feel that their emotions are not taken seriously or acknowledged. If you listen and validate your child's feelings, you will make sure that your child feels accepted and valued as essential to your healing journey.

Below are some methods you can be a good listener and confirm your child's emotions:

Stay present When your child is speaking with you, make sure to be present and provide them with all your attention. It means that you put aside any distracting things like the phone or other activities while focusing at your child.

Make use of active listening skills: Utilize active listening skills, for example, repeating the words your child spoke to you or asking clarification questions. This will show your child you're listening and attempting to understand your perspective.

Recognize their emotions: If your child is feeling upset be sure to validate them by acknowledging the emotions they are feeling and let them know that it's acceptable to be feeling that way. As an example, you could be able to say, "It sounds like you're grieving over what you saw happen. It's totally normal."

Beware of judgment or criticism If your child is expressing their feelings, it's crucial to not judge or critique the way they express their emotions. It can cause them to feel that their feelings do not matter, or that they're accused of being the cause.

www.ingramcontent.com/pod-product-compliance
Lightning Source LLC
Chambersburg PA
CBHW071445080526
44587CB00014B/2004